Thomas St. Edmund Hake

In Letters of Gold

Vol. II

Thomas St. Edmund Hake

In Letters of Gold
Vol. II

ISBN/EAN: 9783337147600

Printed in Europe, USA, Canada, Australia, Japan

Cover: Foto ©ninafisch / pixelio.de

More available books at **www.hansebooks.com**

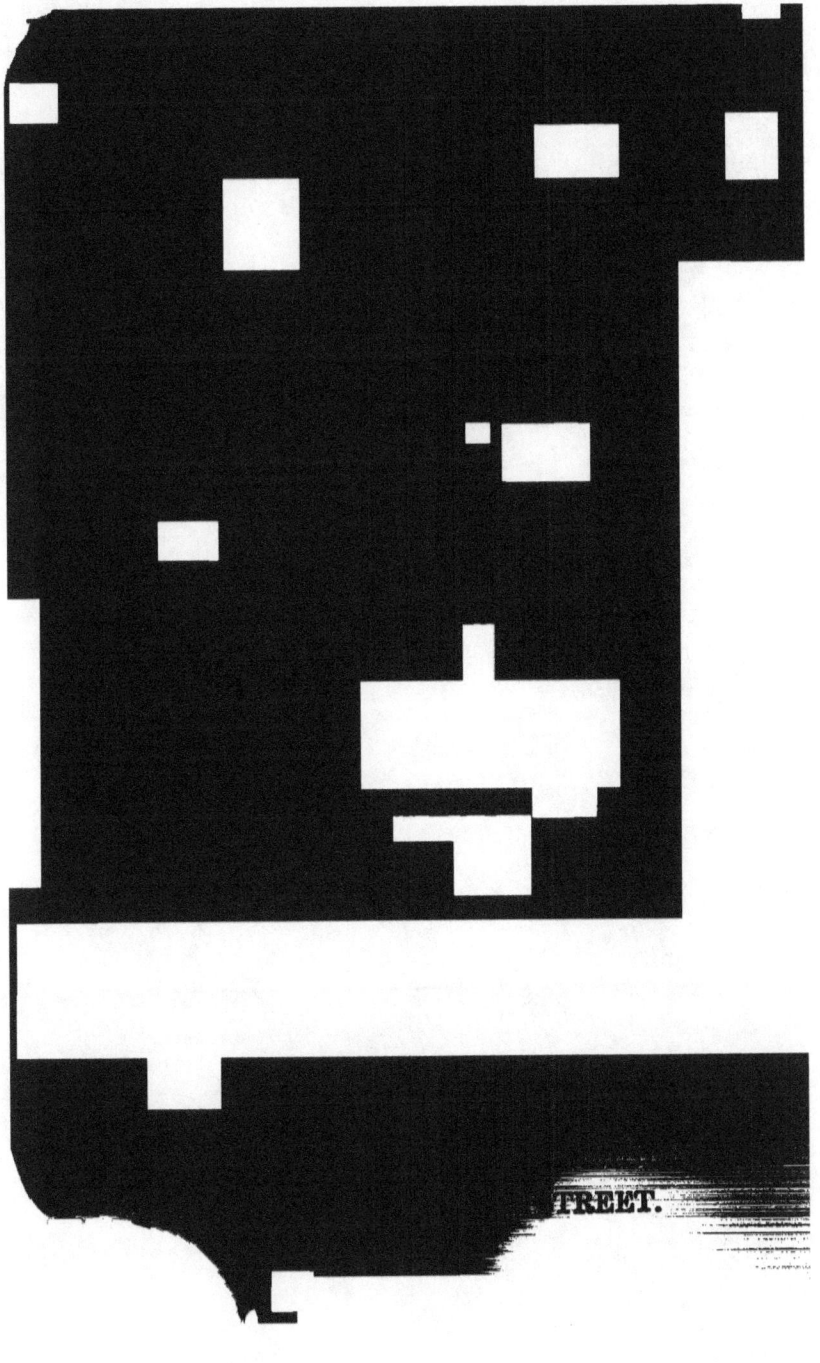

IN LETTERS OF GOLD.

CHAPTER I.

LUDLAW'S SUSPICIONS.

AFTER parting with his 'learned friend,' at the Temple gateway, Ludlaw took the train to Batswing Heath, the large common on the outskirts of London where Sir Michael Valroy lived.

At the time when Ludlaw first became the baronet's legal adviser, some twenty years ago, both he and Sir Michael were newly entering on life. The baronet was rich and well-connected: Ludlaw was comparatively poor and without friends; and his eagerness to gain a position in the world was his avowed reason for showing himself ready and willing to make himself indispensable to others. There happened to be some matters respecting the Valroy estate which required adjustment: Ludlaw proved himself priceless. Then again the baronet became involved in monetary difficulties: once more Ludlaw was consulted, and extricated him with surprising cleverness. For these, and other services, Sir Michael Valroy rewarded Ludlaw with introductions into the best circles; and not only as his friend, but as a keen man of affairs. The lawyer played his cards well: he succeeded in society, while making steady progress in the legal profession.

Seated in a corner of the railway carriage, Ludlaw took from his pocket a letter which he read repeatedly by the dim light overhead. He regarded the writing as one might contemplate a face which had given cause for anger: there was a dark frown on his brow and his thin lips were firmly closed. The letter was from Madame Hélène: it was extremely curt, and ran as follows:

'This delay is maddening. Unless I hear from you at once, I shall consider myself at liberty to act independently in the matter upon which I consulted with you some days ago.'

No one could boast of a more convenient memory than Ludlaw. He had designedly forgotten his promise to intercede with Sir Michael Valroy on behalf of Madame Hélène. He knew enough of her character to be fairly satisfied that she would take no decisive steps before making a final appeal. This left him time to choose a moment most favourable and convenient for approaching the baronet on such a distasteful subject. In Ludlaw's opinion, this affair had only now begun to assume a grave aspect: hitherto it had not been deserving of serious thought. But to venture on further delay would be dangerous. Ludlaw perceived that Madame Hélène was deeply in earnest; and if she visited John Wildrake without the baronet's consent the blame would fall upon him: for he had undertaken to acquaint Sir Michael Valroy with Madame Hélène's resolve to effect a reconciliation between herself and her broken-down father.

On leaving Batswing Heath Station, Ludlaw turned into a narrow way, between high walls, leading towards the common. It was a dark night, and the lamps through this lane were placed some distance apart; so Ludlaw took the precaution of keeping in the centre of the road as he stepped along.

He had frequently walked this way at a later hour. But for some inexplicable reason he experienced on this occasion a feeling of danger foreign to his matter-of-fact nature. Was he in a nervous state? or was it some unforeseen presentiment? He put this question to himself, but without eliciting any satisfactory explanation. All that he could positively declare was that he felt a decided sense of relief when he came to the end of the lane, and reached the open heath.

At this corner, where the roads parted

small country inn. It was the last stage, in the good old times, at which the coaches stopped before entering London. On the green facing the entrance stood a tall white post where the sign-board still swung, and upon which could be seen by the light of the road-lamp, written in old style, 'Ye Hunted Stag.'

As Ludlaw passed the inn he glanced towards the window of the bar-parlour. He noticed two men in the room: the one, standing with his back to the fire, he at once recognised as that of the landlord; the other, seated at a table upon which he was leaning both his arms, appeared to Ludlaw in some remote manner to be well known to him.

But when, or where, had he seen the face?

Curiosity prompted him to stop, and

even turn back. He approached as close to the window as he well could without being observed. Then he looked more attentively at the man. He was talking to the landlord in a low voice. It was impossible to distinguish the words: but from his manner the conversation appeared deeply interesting and earnest. His dress was shabby; a black, thread-bare coat, buttoned tightly round his neck, and a dilapidated old hat. He was smoking a long clay pipe, and a glass of grog was standing at his side upon the table.

Ludlaw searched his memory through a long gallery of faces, dating over a number of eventful years; he threw an inquisitive glance over the past, taking a rapid view of society and of the various courts of justice to recall the name of the man to whom this strangely familiar face belonged. He searched for some moments in vain. But suddenly a peculiar look startled him, and the identification quickly followed. He exclaimed aloud :

'John Wildrake!'

How terribly the face had changed, since he had met Wildrake at Mrs. Aldershaw's receptions in Tyburnia, could only be realised now that the recognition was complete; though to shape out of the red and swollen features a fine, intelligent countenance, such as Ludlaw had had good reason to admire in former days, was no easy task. The brow had grown painfully severe and wrinkled, and the eyebrows shaggy and grey. The eyes had lost their brightness, and the well-formed mouth had become vicious, and was drawn down at the corners into an expression of resentment and scorn.

With something more than mere curiosity now, Ludlaw stepped into the inn. The door of the bar-parlour being open, he could see the two men, while standing outside the bar, without being seen.

A lamp placed upon the mantel-shelf lit up pictures on the walls chiefly of coaches preparing to start at the door of 'Ye Hunted Stag,' or at full speed on the road; there were also pictures of Derby winners, and of celebrated jockeys; altogether, a choice gallery of sport and travel.

The landlord was a tall, shrewd-looking man, closely shaved. He wore tight-fitting breeches, and a coat cut in hunting style, which gave him a somewhat 'racy' appearance. He was eyeing his eccentric-looking customer with some degree of suspicion.

'What you mean is,' Wildrake was saying, 'there have not been many changes in this neighbourhood in your time,—eh, landlord?'

'No changes whatever.'

'No houses sold, eh? No building going on?'

'None,' said the landlord, shortly.

'Nothing about this heath,' Wildrake, suggested, with a jerk of his head, 'except old mansions. And all, I suppose, inhabited by old families?'

'Just that.'

'Been here many years?' Wildrake abruptly demanded.

'A goodish number.'

'In that case,' Wildrake continued, taking a sip at his grog, 'in that case you must be well-acquainted with most of the names of those who live about here?'

'Say all,' replied the landlord, 'every-one of them, and you will be nearer the mark.'

'Ah, now I shouldn't wonder,' said Wildrake, glancing at the landlord knowingly, 'I shouldn't wonder if you could tell, if you chose, some queer stories about one or two. Queer stories, eh?'

'I shouldn't wonder.'

'For instance,' Wildrake remarked, 'that house with the sphinxes on the gates has a queer appearance. You know who lives there, of course?'

'Well,' said the landlord, smiling, 'I ought to know. I was a servant in the family there for twenty years. I left when Sir Michael Valroy, the present baronet, went abroad. I was his father's valet.'

Wildrake again sipped his grog and then said:

'Went abroad, eh? So I've heard.'

'Yes, he went abroad,' said the landlord; 'and we began to think,' he added, 'that Sir Michael never would come back.'

'But he did, eh?'

'Yes. Only a week or so ago.'

Wildrake now rose from his seat, and having paid the reckoning, observed, with a glance towards the window,

'A dark night for a walk, eh, landlord?'

'You'll find it so across the common. Are you going far?'

'To London,' said Wildrake, moving towards the door.

'That's not a long distance,' said the landlord, ' for a man who knows the road.'

'No distance at all,' said Wildrake, hurrying out, though not very steady in his gait. 'Good-night.'

'Good-night,' said the landlord.

Wildrake took no notice of Ludlaw, though he passed close by him. But the barrister hastened on to the door-step and looked after Wildrake keenly: he watched him as he walked away in an unsteady slouching manner, seeming to glance about him to the right and left, and to peer into the gloomy night, like an animal in search of prey. Presently he stopped and appeared to be listening : he struck his chest with his fist, and then started off at a quicker pace, stumbling along the road which led across the common until he disappeared into the darkness.

'Why, Mr. Ludlaw,' said the landlord, 'I thought I couldn't be mistaken. Good-evening, sir.'

'Spicer,' said Ludlaw, turning quickly round, 'do you know the man who has just gone out?'

'No,' said Spicer. 'I've seen him about on the common, once or twice. A strange looking customer, ain't he?'

'He told you just now,' said Ludlaw, 'that he was going to London.'

'Yes. So I understood him.'

'He has taken the opposite direction.'

'Well,' said Spicer, meditatively, 'he did seem one of the sort who don't know their own minds for two minutes together.'

Ludlaw nodded and said:

'Give me one of your choice cigars.'

The landlord hastened to take down a

box from a corner shelf. Ludlaw selected a cigar, lighted it, and smoked for a while in silence. He was still standing at the door of the inn, with his eyes turned towards the direction which Wildrake had taken. Presently he said, with a sudden glance at the landlord:

'Spicer, I have my suspicions.'

'I beg your pardon, sir.'

'Keep an eye,' said Ludlaw, 'upon that man's movements if he comes into this neighbourhood again. He is a notorious character about town.'

'Known, am I to understand, to the police?'

'That's very possible.'

Spicer cocked his head shrewdly on one side.

'You don't surprise me, sir. He looked it from head to foot.'

'How long,' Ludlaw demanded, 'had he been lounging about here.'

'He came in,' said Spicer, 'somewhere near dusk. He ordered a brandy hot: and then he fell asleep in the bar-parlour with his head on the table. I had some difficulty in rousing him, and then I could only keep him awake by talking. He was the worse for drink, I could have sworn, as soon as I caught sight of him.'

'He has the reputation,' said Ludlaw, 'of seldom being sober. Will you let me know if you see him again? I have my grave suspicions.'

'You may rely upon it, sir,' said the landlord of the 'Stag.' 'I shall not forget.'

'Not a word about the man, remember that, to anyone.'

With this admonition, Ludlaw took his

leave, and stepped out quickly across the heath.

Sir Michael Valroy's house lay on the opposite side of the common. Ludlaw chose the path which, as he well knew, led to a point nearest to the gates. It was a dark, lonely walk of nearly a mile, and the thoughts which were passing through the barrister's mind with regard to John Wildrake did not assist to dissipate the effect of the surrounding gloom. A vast shadow, as it seemed, was hanging overhead; while along the roads, which intersected the heath, the lamps with their small, glimmering circles of light gave a wider and deeper expansion to the darkness.

The appearance of Wildrake in this neighbourhood could, as it appeared to Ludlaw, be no mere coincidence. He had evidently some fixed purpose in visiting the 'Hunted Stag:' some strong design in questioning the landlord about the return of Sir Michael Valroy from abroad. His reference to 'the house with the sphinxes on the gates' indicated clearly that his thoughts were directed towards the baronet.

But what could be his motive? If Wildrake suspected Sir Michael Valroy of having led his daughter astray, and had waited all these years for his coming home in order to confront and question him, it was indeed time that an explanation of the whole affair was accorded him. By obtaining Sir Michael's consent to a meeting between Madame Hélène and her father this desirable end would be achieved. This was all supposition on Ludlaw's part: but he resolved to seize upon this incident as affording the most irrefutable argument in favour of a reconciliation.

In the midst of these reflections he reached the park entrance to Sir Michael Valroy's mansion. Standing at the gates, while the lodge-keeper answered the bell, he happened to glance up at the two stern, stoney-faced sphinxes reposing there with lamps on pedestals behind them: and the shadows which flitted across their solemn features suggested the ludicrous thought to Ludlaw's mind that the one was whispering to the other about the mysteries of coming events which concerned the house of Valroy.

Upon the same evening, an hour later, Ludlaw was seated among the family portraits, in the old dining-hall, facing Sir Michael Valroy.

Sir Michael, who leant his elbow on the table, with his head resting upon his hand, looked sternly at the barrister. He had by nature a severe expression, black, cruel eyes, and a heavy brow. His dark beard was slightly tinged with grey. He was a large, powerfully-built man: and against the light of the shaded lamp behind him he appeared almost gigantic.

'You have something to communicate, Ludlaw,' he remarked. 'Why don't you speak?'

'Drink another glass of wine first,' Ludlaw replied, glancing towards the decanters. 'Your nerves may require stimulating.'

The baronet rejected this friendly counsel with an angry gesture of the hand.

'I am the bearer of a message.'

'To me?'

'Yes,' said Ludlaw; 'and the message is from your wife, Lady Valroy. She is in London.'

'What?'

'I was honoured with a visit from her, at Pump Court, a day or two ago,' Ludlaw continued. 'Lady Valroy introduced herself as an old client who had come to ask, as a matter of business, my legal advice. She has petitioned me to intercede with you on her behalf. May I state the case?'

'Is it worth while?'

'Yes. Lady Valroy, after years of uncomplaining submission to the terms expressed in an agreement between her and yourself, begs leave to have the contract annulled. I refer,' Ludlaw explained, 'to the one entered into immediately prior to your marriage. The conditions of that contract were that Helen Wildrake should, when married, cease to hold any communication with her father, John Wildrake, without the sanction of Sir Michael Valroy.'

'Is the woman mad?'

'Lady Valroy begs leave,' pursued Ludlaw, 'to resume relations with the said father. She has heard indirectly that he has taken to drink, and has fallen into a state of destitution, and she believes that her undutiful conduct is the cause of it. She is full of repentance, and eager to make amends.'

Sir Michael Valroy had risen from his seat, while Ludlaw was still speaking, and commenced pacing to and fro. He now stopped, and answered, in a firm and angry voice,

'Tell her,' said he, 'that I insist upon her adherring to the terms mentioned in the deed which was drawn up by you before our marriage. I will never give my consent to a meeting between her and her father. My motive in exacting that agreement was, as you know, in order to provide against the possibility of having to discuss the matter at some future time. No sentimental talk about her father's destitution will have any effect with me. On the contrary, it confirms me in my decision, and strengthens me in my resolution not to yield one jot.'

He paused and looked at Ludlaw fixedly, as though expecting some reply; but, receiving none, he continued:

'I know John Wildrake of old. I foresaw, before I married his daughter, that he would end his days in drink. It was on that man's account that I determined to keep my marriage secret. I never considered the connection as otherwise than most disreputable. Is my wife anxious,' he fiercely demanded, 'to be known in every low tavern in London as Lady Valroy?'

'For your sake,' said Ludlaw, 'I am confident she would take every precaution to prevent a scandal.'

'No precaution will keep silent a drunkard's tongue,' said Sir Michael Valroy. 'But why,' he added, 'why waste time in discussing the matter? I shall not alter my decision.'

'In that case,' said Ludlaw, 'I have something to propose. It may prevent Lady Valroy from acting in a mad, impulsive manner, as I fear she will, when I acquaint her with your sentiments.'

'What is your suggestion?'

'Consent,' said Ludlaw, 'to an interview with Lady Valroy.'

A black look crossed the baronet's face.

'At Pump Court,' added Ludlaw, persuasively, 'and in my presence.'

'As a matter of business?'

'Precisely.'

'No emotional nonsense?'

'I will guarantee that.'

'Well, then,' said Sir Michael, reluctantly, 'I'll agree.'

'When?'

'The sooner,' the baronet replied, 'the better.'

Then he resumed his pacing to and fro. Suddenly he stepped towards the door.

'I am going,' said he, 'for a sharp walk across the heath. I feel restless, and out of sorts.'

Ludlaw looked up with a start.

'To-night?'

The baronet observed this change of manner with suspicion.

'Why not?' said he. 'Do you know of any reason?'

'Yes.'

'You surprise me.'

'I came this evening,' said Ludlaw, 'past "The Hunted Stag." In the bar-parlour of the inn I saw John Wildrake. I am convinced that he is prowling about on the common at this very hour.'

'What then?'

'In your present mood,' said Ludlaw, 'I need scarcely remind you that it would be better that you should not encounter that man. He has probably been suspecting you, all these years, of knowing something about his daughter's disappearance.'

'If we meet,' said Sir Michael Valroy, with an angry flash in his eyes, 'and he questions me, he shall have his answer. I promise him that!'

With these words he went out. Ludlaw heard his quick footstep as he crossed the hall; and then the loud slam of the front door sounded in the barister's ear, and shook the very walls of the old mansion.

It cannot be said that Ludlaw's sense of uneasiness, if he felt any regarding Sir Michael Valroy, lasted many minutes after the baronet had left the room. The barrister was a man of cool reflection, accustomed to look upon the business of life as a disagreeable necessity of circumstance. Besides, he had dined well at the baronet's table, and a certain feeling of drowsiness began to overtake him when he found himself alone: so he drew his chair closer to the fire, and, covering his face with his handkerchief, presently fell into a comfortable doze. The ticking of the clock on the mantel-shelf once more kept pace with his breathing, and then ran ahead as it had frequently done before: and the old portraits of the Valroy family, upon whose faces there seemed to be a settled expression of gloom, looked dismally down upon the barrister, as he sat there sleeping as though in disapproval of his presumption, as a visitor, in affecting such a very cosy attitude in one of the ancestral armchairs.

An hour passed—two hours.

Meanwhile Ludlaw had a strange dream.

He dreamt that he was seated over the hearth, in the chambers at Pump Court, and that the lamp gradually grew dimmer and dimmer, until at last he was left in darkness. Then he dreamt that he got up slowly from his chair and groped his way through the bed-room in search of a light, and that, finding none, he came back by the passage, where all was equally dark, and again entered his study. As he pushed open the door he observed a tall white figure, with the face of Lady Valroy, standing behind his chair; one hand was raised over her heart as though to protect it, and with the other she pointed towards a chair on the opposite side of the chimney-corner: glancing in that direction he perceived Sir Michael

Valroy with a pistol, which he was aiming towards the figure; suddenly he pulled the trigger, and the report of the pistol rang through the chambers.

Ludlaw started and awoke.

Snatching the handkerchief from his face he looked in bewilderment around him. For a moment he still imagined himself in the study at Pump Court; for the first object that caught his attention was Sir Michael Valroy standing near the dining-hall door, with a face as pale as death.

'What's happened?'

The baronet did not at once reply. He stepped towards the fire and sank down in a chair. As he plucked nervously at his beard, Ludlaw remarked that there was a stain, in colour resembling blood, on the back of Sir Michael Valroy's hand. The baronet's eye followed Ludlaw's glance.'

'I have met him,' said he.

'Who?'

'John Wildrake,' said Sir Michael Valroy.

CHAPTER II.

DEGRADED.

On Batswing Heath, at a point where two roads meet, there is a sign-post at one corner. Opposite to it stands a lamp. The light from this lamp, illuminating a limited space, fell upon a prostrate figure lying motionless beneath the sign-post, face downward.

It had become such a gloomy night that the clouds overhead lowered until they were almost on a level with the ground: a night so ponderous and opaque that not even a gleam of light stole in from any point of the horizon; there was not upon this broad expanse of common one ray to help the expression of lingering day or coming dawn. The four arms of the sign-post pointed to black shadows; they seemed to indicate that a mystery was in this darkness to be discovered in the sombre ways across the heath.

Presently the figure moved, and a ghastly face was raised towards the lamp. It was the face of John Wildrake.

The old clerk lifted himself upon his elbow, and glanced about him into the night. Suddenly he seemed to gain some recollection of where he was; for he threw himself once more upon his face with a deep groan, as if to shut out the remembrance.

'I asked him for my daughter,' he

moaned, 'I asked him to give her back to me, and he struck me down.'

For a moment he lay quite still.

'The blow,' he muttered, in a piteous tone, 'the blow has stunned me.'

Then he crept feebly towards the sign-post, and leant his back against it, and passed his hand across his forehead. He was trembling violently. But there was a look of fierce resentment gathering over his features; his teeth were set with the ferocity of an injured animal; he was staring with stoney fixedness, as though at some mental spectre, with a strange and deadly hatred in his eyes.

He had been struck down. The degrading truth had awakened a latent energy in the man. A dogged purpose had seized upon his senses, and it had taken such a strong hold upon his nature that he submitted with readiness, stubbornly resolved to put all reflection on one side, and yield himself up to the impulse.

In the distance, along the cross-road running east and west, a carriage was advancing at a quick pace; the carriage lamps flashed into the night, and the tramping of the horses' hoofs sounded every moment louder in Wildrake's ear.

He tried to get upon his legs, but fell back helplessly.

His face grew pale and still more expressive of retaliation. He shook from head to foot, as though attacked by a violent fit of ague; he uttered a savage imprecation, between his chattering teeth, in a deep and agonising tone. His voice became hoarse with a passion which seemed like the ravings of a madman: and then he fell over once more, a motionless figure, with his face to the ground.

The carriage drew nearer: it soon reached the four cross-roads. As it was passing the sign-post a man's head appeared at the carriage-window, and a voice cried out:

'Stop!'

The carriage came to a standstill. A footman descended and stood at the carriage-door.

'There is some one lying there. See what has happened.'

The servant stepped towards Wildrake, and questioned him. He moved, and answered:

'I have been struck down.'

The gentleman at the carriage window demanded:

'Where do you live?'

'In London.'

'Do you wish to go there?'

'Yes.'

There was a short silence.

'Help the man to rise.'

The servant obeyed.

Wildrake staggered forward and stopped, passing his hand nervously over his face.

'Can you walk?' the gentleman inquired.

'Not a step,' said Wildrake, feebly, 'not to save my life.'

'Get in, then, beside me. I am going to London.'

Wildrake looked bewildered.

'Take a seat in your carriage?'

'Yes. That is what I offer you.'

The old clerk came slowly forward, with

his hand resting for support on the servant's shoulder.

'I am deeply obliged,' said he, in a low voice.

He was soon assisted into the carriage, and the horses started off along their road. During the drive not a word passed between Wildrake and his unknown benefactor. The old clerk had squeezed himself into a corner of the carriage: and he sat there with folded arms, and with his head bent low. The dogged purpose which possessed him was doing active work within his brain: and although more than once a shudder passed over him, at the vividness and horror of his own thoughts, there were no signs of a disposition to falter. His attitude was one of unswerving resolution to vindicate the injuries of which he was not the only victim.

The dark common was soon left behind. Passing along a well-lighted road, the carriage crossed a bridge over the Thames, and presently came in sight of the great clock-tower at Westminster. London was now reached; and after driving along Whitehall, and through the Strand, the carriage drew up at the Temple gateway.

'Are you better?'

'Yes. I can walk now,' said Wildrake, stepping out slowly,—'I can walk now. I am deeply obliged to you. Goodnight.'

Then Wildrake moved away, with the strange, hasty manner of a blind man groping his way along a familiar road.

The gentleman, standing on the pavement, watched him attentively as he went down Fleet Street in the direction of the City, and gradually became indistinguishable in the crowd: he then turned round to address the servant, and his face became visible. It was Ludlaw.

'I shall want you,' said he, 'to take back a letter to Sir Michael. Step up with me to the chambers. The letter must be delivered into his hands to-night.'

The barrister led the way. As he mounted the stairs in Pump Court, he was reminded of the unpleasant dream he had had that very evening while awaiting Sir Michael Valroy's return from his walk upon Batswing Heath. On entering the chambers a cold sensation crept over him, and he hastened to light the lamp and dispel the passing fancy of a white figure standing behind his arm-chair. The events of the day had affected his nerves.

Seating himself at his desk, Ludlaw wrote to Sir Michael as follows :

'My principal object in borrowing your carriage to-night was to convey Wildrake to London. I found him lying at the crossroads where, in your passion, you knocked him down. He had sufficiently recovered his strength when we reached Fleet Street to be able to walk home. By this I am greatly relieved : for I had no wish to be retained for your defence in a case in which no display of eloquent pleading could have secured you a favourable verdict.'

Having dismissed the servant with this note to the baronet in token of reproof, Ludlaw fell into a meditation over the delicate question of Sir Michael and Lady Valroy's 'agreement,' which was shortly to be discussed between them in his presence.

Wildrake, in the meantime, making his way along Fleet Street, came to the turning which led towards the Loafers' Hall. At that moment a number of 'loafers' were leaving the tavern; for it was past midnight, and the doors were being closed. The talking and laughter was loud and riotous: a hubbub of voices, among which only stray words and broken sentences reached his ear. At sight of these men, Wildrake shrank back with a sudden apprehension of being recognised, and sought shelter within the shadow of a doorway to let this noisy crowd pass. For coarse companionship and revelry had apparently no longer any interest for him:

he even seemed to fear that this change which had come over him within the last few hours should be read in his face and bring down upon him insult and jeers. His attitude, as he stood there looking out from his hiding-place, was that of a man who contemplates committing a crime and who dreads observation.

These 'loafers' having dispersed at last, he crept guiltily forth to continue on his road homeward. He had not proceeded many steps before he heard some one walking behind him at a quick pace. He glanced round nervously, and found himself face to face with Nedlicott.

Mr. Cheadle's secretary, returning home from the 'Frivolity,' was on the look-out for Wildrake, who so often needed his assistance about this hour. He was surprised to see him standing there so steady before him. He regarded the old clerk more closely. He then noticed that his forehead was swollen between the eyebrows, and that there were marks of blood on his pale face.

But something in the man's expression most attracted Nedlicott's attention. It startled him.

'What's the matter?' he exclaimed. 'You are terribly changed. What ails you, Wildrake?'

'Don't question me now,' Wildrake answered, in a low, hurried tone. 'Give me your arm, Ned. Help me to get home.'

'What have you been drinking?'

'Nothing.'

'What?'

'Not a drop. On my honour, Ned, not a drop.'

'You come from the "Loafers." Don't you?'

'No. That is all ended,' said Wildrake, 'all ended now.'

Leaning upon Nedlicott's arm, he moved along in silence. It was a slow pace, but, unlike his usual loitering, steady and decisive. There was no apparent disposition to stop on his way to-night at favourite corners, nor to sink upon convenient doorsteps as a place for 'rest:' no plaintive demands for 'sleep' escaped his lips: there seemed indeed a wakefulness and a force in his manner which Nedlicott, in the years he had known Wildrake, had no recollection of witnessing before. But, what seemed most surprising, he made no reference to his lost daughter: he showed no signs of being disturbed by her footsteps: he did not even listen for that haunting sound. But was not something else, something even more serious than that, haunting him on his way home to-night? A black look, like a shadow, was stamped upon his face: his eyes, as though bent upon this something in his path, were fixed and full of anger.

Turning at last out of Thames Street, through the open gateway, they entered the old courtyard. But it was not until Wildrake stood upon his doorstep under the dim lamp that he addressed a word to Nedlicott, or even gave any indication that he was conscious of his presence, though leaning upon his arm. He then disengaged himself, and twisted round, as though he had been suddenly roused by a passing thought.

'Ned,' said he, clenching his fist and

clutching with his other hand the iron railing, 'I've been struck down.'

'How's that?'

Wildrake pointed energetically across the dark river.

'Out there,' he cried, in excitement—'out there, upon the heath, I have met to-night the man I've been waiting to meet for fifteen years—ay, Nedlicott, more than fifteen years—the man who has brought all this trouble upon me—who has made me what you see me now, a poor, miserable drunkard.'

His quick, angry utterance half stifled him; but, after a moment of silence, he recovered breath.

'I watched,' said he, 'and watched for his return to England until I nearly lost all hope. If I have crossed that heath once during those long years, I have crossed it a thousand times. It was always the same answer when I made inquiries—"still abroad." Sometimes, in my great anxiety and doubt, I have lain down under the shadow of his gates, like a common tramp, all night long. For I had a sort of notion,' added Wildrake, lowering his voice, 'that she, my daughter, might come that way. It was there, at those gates, that her footstep sounded most distinctly—always at those gates.'

He paused with a grief-stricken look in his face

'Since we've met—since that man and I have met again, face to face,' Wildrake quickly resumed, 'her footstep has ceased to torment me. What torments me now is his voice: his words still ring in my ear. I see his face still, and his uplifted arm—his arm raised against me, Nedlicott, against me. He insulted me, and then struck me down.'

'Who?'

Wildrake, instead of replying, passed his trembling hands in his bewildered way across his forehead. Then he looked piteously at Nedlicott.

'The man that robbed me of my daughter,' said he at last, in a subdued and shaky tone—'it is of him that I am speaking; and to-night, crossing the heath once more, I found out that he had returned. I even learnt that he was in the habit of taking walks upon the common after dark. No time, no place could be better, as it seemed to me, in which to accost him and demand what had become of her. I waited about for hours in an agony of expectation. It seemed so long that I began to fear that I should see a streak of light in the east, as I had so often done, and not have encountered him.'

Wildrake's manner, for a moment, became thoughtful; he appeared to be recalling to mind those tedious hours. But presently he glanced up again with a flash of anger in his face.

'But he came at last,' cried he, 'came suddenly upon me at the cross-roads, and I placed myself straight in his path. I could see by his look that he recognised me, before I uttered one word. He stopped, and retreated a step: and then I spoke and implored him to give my daughter back to me, if she was still alive. He answered, with an oath, that he knew nothing about the " woman," and he ordered me, in an insolent tone, to get out of his way. But I stood my ground: and then words, which it makes my brain burn to think of, passed between us. His passion was more furious than mine. At last he sprang at me and struck me in the face with his fist, and I fell back stunned!'

These words, though scarcely spoken above a whisper, were uttered with surprising energy, and when Wildrake ceased his lips still trembled and his face was white with rage.

Nedlicott, greatly alarmed about the old clerk, placed his hand upon his shoulder and tried to soothe him.

'Wildrake,' said he, 'you are working yourself into a fever. Do not do that. You have been insulted, grossly, I am ready to admit. But this outburst of anger will not mend matters between you and this man. When you are calmer, we will talk about this again. Whether you have acted wisely in choosing a dark and a lonely spot to settle such a serious affair I will not discuss. It is late, and you are too feverish to-night.'

'Ned,' replied Wildrake, in a strange tone, 'do you think that any man, who has suffered such treatment as I have suffered, can ever get calmer?'

'Yes, he should,' said Nedlicott: 'if he would only reflect.'

'Should he? why?' answered Wildrake, with vehemence; 'the more I reflect, the more incensed I am against the man: I seem to see more clearly every moment what a heartless villain he is. Don't ask me to reflect. I am already driven mad with that!'

In his agony of mind he sank against the railings, and his head dropped upon his arms. Nedlicott tried every means to persuade him to go in, and get the rest which he never needed more, never more than now. He spoke to him kindly: he spoke to him in a severe tone; but no words wonld move him. He never changed his attitude, nor uttered one syllable in reply to his friend's eloquent remonstrance.

So long did Wildrake remain motionless there, with his head upon the railings, that when he looked up and stared about him he missed Nedlicott. Was he gone? He listened. No sound reached his ear except that endless lapping of the tide in the shadows under the wharves beyond the dark court-yard: for the old city was still sleeping, and the black night still covered every corner of the sky.

Wildrake's face, as he glanced searchingly around, became once more full of wakefulness and energy; his features were even more emphatically marked with that expression of intenseness and stubborn purpose which had sprung into them, like an inspiration, as he lay helpless upon Batswing Heath. He had the appearance of a man who, when haunted by one overpowering motive, excludes every other impulse or thought: for he no longer groaned, or leant for support against the broken spikes of the old mansion; he stood up a firm and resolute figure, with some show of nervous force in all his limbs.

Presently he moved softly across Gable Court, and walked towards the river. For a while he lingered there, like the ebbing tide, in the deep gloom under a great warehouse: he stood quite still, looking intently over the 'silent highway' into the blackness beyond.

All of a sudden he turned and fled with a low cry upon his lips: his step was noiseless, but hurried, as though he were terror-stricken by something he had seen, something more dreadful than he could find courage to face, even as a mere creation of his own heated brain.

He reached the doorstep, and hastened to let himself in to the sombre old hall. The place looked more gloomy than usual; for the little oil lamp, in its retired corner, was on the point of expiring.

Groping his way towards his candle, which stood upon a table near the foot of the staircase, Wildrake applied it to this dying flame; he had no sooner lighted it than the lamp spluttered feebly and went out.

Wildrake raised his candle, and, shading it with his hand, he peered about cautiously before ascending the stairs. As he looked around him, his eyes fell upon two massive tablets, belonging to the old Jew, containing the ten commandments. A startled look came into his eyes, and he caught his breath as though he had received a mortal stab.

The shadow of his hand was trembling over these words, written in letters of gold:

Thou shalt do no murder.

He staggered and fell back heavily against the wall; the candlestick dropped from his fingers, clattering upon the stone floor, and he was left in darkness.

CHAPTER III.

FAINT HEARTS.

'TEDDIE,' said Mrs. Nedlicott, stepping one evening out of the shop into the little parlour, 'it's five o'clock.'

The room was very sombre, for December was advancing. Besides, this cosy retreat never had been famous for its sunny aspect, even at noon on a midsummer's day; for a great warehouse at the back had doomed that side of the house to lasting shadows.

'Strike a light, mother,' said Nedlicott,

'and give us a cup of tea. I must be off soon.'

He had been taking an afternoon nap in anticipation of late hours at the 'Frivolity Theatre.'

When the candle was lighted, Mr. Cheadle's secretary found that during his nap the table had been laid, and that the kettle was now singing cheerfully on the hob.

'Why!' said he, putting his arm playfully round his mother's waist, 'what a good soul you are! You're always looking after your son's comfort, ain't you?'

'Ah!' sighed Mrs. Nedlicott, 'it won't be for long.'

'Not for long?' echoed the son, seating himself at the table. 'I don't know what you mean, mother. You're not going to die yet, are you?'

Mrs. Nedlicott sat down opposite to her son and began to pour out the tea.

'Ah! Teddie, I can see!' said she, with a meaning glance at her son, 'I can see, my dear, plainly enough.'

'I've no doubt you can,' said Nedlicott, laughing. 'Your eyes are still as bright, I'll be bound, as ever they were. What then?'

'Nothing,' replied the widow, evasively; 'all I mean to say is that young men who have been in the habit of resting at home on the Sabbath don't spend their Sunday evenings away from home without a reason. I repeat, my dear, it won't be for long. You are going to leave me.'

'Why, mother,' began Nedlicott, 'I thought you knew my reason . . .'

'There was a time, Teddie,' interrupted Mrs. Nedlicott, 'when you were pleased, as I thought, to devote the only spare evening that you have in the week to me.'

'And so I should be now,' said Nedlicott, earnestly. 'But it so happens that, being engaged every night at the Frivolity, I am obliged to choose Sunday for calling upon Mr. Snowby. Otherwise I should never be able to see him; and . . .'

'There was a time,' repeated Mrs. Nedlicott, 'when I thought that you were not only pleased, but happy and contented with my society. But I suppose,' the widow added, resignedly, 'that the subjects requiring discussion between you and Mr. Snowby are more to your taste. Is the man writing a drama?'

'My dear mother,' said Nedlicott, with earnestness, 'the subject discussed between us—as you know very well—the subject of mutual interest is John Wildrake. We have great hope of rescuing him from his miserable condition.'

'That,' said Mrs. Nedlicott, 'is all very well: highly meritorious and philanthropic. But you won't make me believe, Teddie, that two men ever found it worth their while to spend a whole evening once a week in talking about nothing else except a poor, old, broken-down individual like Mr. Wildrake. There are other reasons, my dear, other reasons. Didn't you tell me, some weeks ago, that Mr. Snowby had a daughter?'

'I may,' said Nedlicott, stooping down to light his pipe at the fire, 'have mentioned the fact.'

The exertion brought a rush of colour to his cheeks.

'Ah, Teddie,' said the mother, 'you not

only mentioned the fact; you told me, if I am not mistaken, that she was very pretty. You spoke, indeed, of her beautiful nature, her cheerful disposition, and her deep affection for her father. You were so eloquent in her praise upon that occasion that I began at once to have my suspicions.'

'Why, mother,' said Nedlicott, blowing aside a cloud of tobacco, 'what on earth could you suspect?'

'I began to suspect,' said Mrs. Nedlicott, 'that you had fallen in love.'

Nedlicott commenced knocking the ashes vigorously out of his pipe.

'Just like you,' said he, 'always getting some nonsense of that sort into your old head about me.'

'I began to suspect,' reiterated his mother, 'that all the talk with Mr. Snowby about this unfortunate old clerk was not altogether the cause of my son's arm-chair being empty every Sunday evening. I began to suspect that it was somebody else who was robbing me of his society—somebody with a sweet voice and laughing eyes.'

Nedlicott made no reply. He went on smoking pensively.

'And many an evening,' continued the widow, 'when seated here alone by the fireside, especially of a Sunday evening, I have thought to myself the time is coming now when Teddie will leave me for good. He has found some one who will make for him a happier home than a mother can ever hope to do: a brighter and a happier home.'

Still Nedlicott was silent.

'It's the way of the world,' Mrs. Nedlicott admitted, 'it's the way of the world. And nobody shall say that I was not prepared to bear resignedly and even with cheerfulness any deprivation which might add to my son's happiness. But why, I have sometimes wondered, why doesn't he take his mother into his confidence? He knows how ready she has always been to participate in all his joys and sorrows ever since he was a boy. That's what is hurting her feelings. She doesn't like being treated as a stranger.'

Nedlicott laid down his pipe and held out his hand in his frank manner.

'Forgive me, mother,' said he, 'I am a selfish, ungrateful son. But somehow I never could pluck up the courage to tell you plainly what is only too true, that I love Kate Snowby. I love her more deeply than I can well express. It is a mad, hopeless passion, for I don't believe that I have the slightest chance of winning her. She is everything that is good and beautiful: far too good, and far too beautiful, to ever care for an ordinary chap like me. Why, she is my superior in every respect: in nobleness of character, in education, and in social position. I'm only a handy man at a West-End show, with a few pounds a week. It's not good enough, mother. It would not provide a suitable home for such an angel.'

The mother looked thoughtfully into her son's face.

'If she loves you,' said the widow, 'she would consent to live in a garret. But you are misrepresenting yourself, my dear, and your affairs. The salary you receive from Mr. Cheadle is by no means despicable; and, as for your social position, your father was a gentleman born and bred. A dispensing chemist in Shoreditch is as good as a City clerk any day. And that is all Mr. Snowby is—a clerk in the City.'

'Mr. Snowby,' said Nedlicott, 'is only a clerk at present. But he is a clerk in the great house of Aldershaw, Grimwade and Company. His prospects are brilliant. He told me, only last Sunday, that there was every likelihood of his being taken into partnership at an early date; in fact, that it was only a question of dusting and re-decorating the late Mr. Grimwade's private office, which has been unoccupied for half-a-century. Mr. Snowby will some day be a millionaire; and it is his intention to choose a husband for his daughter among the best ranks of society.'

'That' said Mrs. Nedlicott, 'sounds to me very foolish. An unequal match often brings misery. Miss Snowby, from what you tell me, must be a quiet, homely girl. She does not want an aristocratic husband. She is the sort of woman to make a steady, hard-working man, like my son, an excellent wife.'

'Much too good for me, mother,' persisted Nedlicott, 'much too good for me.'

'Faint heart,' said the old-fashioned widow, 'never won fair lady. Mr. Snowby must like you, or else he would never have invited you to his house. And if his daughter,' added Mrs. Nedlicott, 'has not already seen some loveable qualities in my son, she is not the quick, bright-eyed girl he has described her to be. I am quite sure of that.'

Nedlicott rose from his seat and embraced his mother with unusual vigour. He then put on his hat and overcoat; and with the indispensable prompter's copy, in the brown-paper cover, under his arm, the secretary started off for the Frivolity Theatre with a lighter step and a more hopeful look on his face.

Owing to active preparations for the production of Mr. Cheadle's new comedy, 'Nobs,' Nedlicott had lately been too busy to visit Wildrake. Since the night upon which he had perplexed the secretary by his plaintive story of having at last encountered the man who had robbed him of his daughter, nothing Nedlicott was told had been heard of him at the Loafers' Tavern. He had forsaken his old haunts. This appeared to Nedlicott somewhat strange. Yet he saw no cause for alarm:

he relied upon Wildrake's landlord, who was ever ready to step over to the little shop to lodge complaints against the 'bad one' upon the slightest provocation. It was, therefore, more from a sense of curiosity than from disquietude that the secretary now turned into the dark courtyard, on his way through Thames Street, and mounted the worn steps of the dismal mansion to learn news of the old clerk.

By the light of the little oil lamp, in the corner of the hall, Nedlicott noticed a mysterious expression on Mr. Isaac's face when he had let him in, and had softly closed the door.

'Mr. Nedlicott,' whispered the Jew. 'Did you ever know such a change? He's not the same man.'

'You refer to Wildrake.'

The Jew nodded.

'You find, perhaps,' Nedlicott hinted, 'that he is less unruly than he was?'

'Why,' said Mr. Isaacs, 'that's just where it is! I can't accuse him of being unruly any longer. I wish I could; for I liked him better when he was a bad one than I do now. I liked him much better, Mr. Nedlicott, very much better.'

'It is some days,' said Nedlicott, 'since I have seen Wildrake.'

'In that case,' said the Jew, 'you would scarcely know him.'

'Is he at home?'

'No. He creeps out now, every evening, as soon as it begins to get dark. Just before daylight he returns.'

'Drunk, or sober?'

'Perfectly sober. He never touches a drop,' said the Jew, 'and he never speaks to anyone; he goes about like a man in his sleep. It makes my blood crawl to look at him. He stares vacantly before him, as though he were blind. It's my opinion, Mr. Nedlicott, that he is getting weak-headed. And he must be weak in the legs, too,' added Mr. Isaacs, ' for he carries a thick oaken stick about with him wherever he goes.'

Nedlicott cautiously inquired :

' How do you explain this change ?'

' I can in no way account for it,' was the reply.

' Does he never listen now,' said the secretary, ' for his daughter's footsteps ?'

' Never. That craziness has left him.'

' This, then,' said Nedlicott, ' must be a new form of mania.'

' Yes ; and one,' persisted the Jew, ' that I don't like the looks of. His sottish ways were comprehensible ; but when a man is so secret and so queer, I don't know what to make of it at all.'

Nedlicott endeavoured to reassure the old Jew. He declared that Wildrake's friends were showing signs of recognition: that there was even some talk of providing him with a suitable home.

'The sooner the better,' said Mr. Isaacs, as Nedlicott moved towards the door—'the sooner the better. Let them pay his rent, so long in arrears, and take him away. If I don't get rid of him, he will, some day, drive me as crazy as himself.'

In a small room behind the scenes at the 'Frivolity,' an hour later, sits Mr. Cheadle's secretary. The noise of hammering and scene-shifting strikes incessantly upon the ear. It is the first night of 'Nobs,' Mr. Cheadle's new comedy, and Nedlicott is overwhelmed with work. His door is as constantly opened and shut as a steam-valve, letting in the head of an actor, a scene-shifter, or the call-boy: a question is asked, and answered, and the head vanishes, and another appears. In the midst of this bustle and interruption, Nedlicott gives and receives instructions with the coolness of a sea-captain getting his ship under weigh.

Presently in walks Mr. Cheadle.

'Want me, Nedlicott?'

No. Mr. Cheadle is not in requisition.

'Pennethorne all right?'

Yes: perfectly recovered.

'And Thornycroft?'

Never better in her life.

'If you should want me,' says the dramatist, impressively, 'you'll find me in front of the house. I shall stop there until it's time to ring up.'

Mr. Cheadle disappears down a dark staircase, and, passing along a narrow passage, enters by a private way the corridor of the theatre. In the saloon he encounters Roy Valroy.

'Why,' exclaims the dramatist, 'it's my hero!'

He shakes Valroy cordially by the hand.

'You're the very man,' he adds, 'that I wanted to see.'

Mr. Cheadle takes his hero's arm and leads him into the smoking-room.

'Let me congratulate you,' says he, 'upon the admirable manner in which you are playing your part. When do you leave England?'

They are seated face to face in a quiet corner.

'To-night,' says Valroy.

'You could not,' Mr. Cheadle asserts, 'have chosen—from a dramatic point of view—a more opportune moment.'

'Why so?'

'Because,' remarks the dramatist, 'Dwyver stands out prominently to-night as your rival. The scene takes place at Lord Mounthaw's house in Palace Gardens.'

'Is Marion going to Lady Mounthaw's this evening?'

'Precisely! Enter Marion Aldershaw and the merchant. Aristocratic crowd in the background. Dwyver steps on to the scene. Dialogue between heroine and rival. Merchant looks on delighted. In this scene the hero does not appear.'

A look of trouble crosses Valroy's face.

'All is at an end,' he declares, 'between Marion and myself.'

'Yes—for the present,' says Mr. Cheadle, 'quite right. That idea was admirably carried out in the scene which took place in my drawing-room at Chelsea. It was very effective—from a dramatic point of view—very effective indeed. But, don't forget, the last act remains to be played. A year—perhaps two years—may elapse. That is a mere matter of detail.'

Valroy rises and holds out his hand.

'Good-bye, Cheadle,' says he, 'I shall never come back to England.'

'Never? That would spoil the comedy!'

'I am serious.'

'But, my dear Valroy, you must,' Mr. Cheadle insists; 'you must take the lead in the last act. I shall count upon you. Is it not the very situation—from a dramatic point of view—which we want to complete the comedy? Return of hero from abroad —tableau—curtain!'

With this the two men part. Roy Valroy, who cannot be induced to remain, leaves the theatre, and Mr. Cheadle hurries to his private box to witness the rise of the curtain upon his new comedy. The comedy is a great success; roars of laughter from first to last. The curtain falls amidst great applause. There are cries of 'author!' on every side. Mr. Cheadle leaves his box and arrives at the wings by the narrow passage. Nedlicott is standing in readiness with a corner of the stage curtain in his hand which he holds back for the dramatist. A perfect ovation greets the author as he appears before the footlights. But Mr. Cheadle, to whom these flattering signs of popular recognition are matters of constant occurence, bows his acknowledgements as a mere duty without any show of emotion beyond a jovial smile.

It was late that night before Nedlicott turned his steps homeward. It being a musical evening at the 'Fresco,' he lingered at that artistic club to learn the various opinions of his theatrical friends about Mr. Cheadle's comedy, and to receive congratulations upon the manner in which he had placed the play upon the 'boards.' Besides, he had to take his seat at the supper-table with some of the members of the Frivolity company—an invariable custom upon first nights; nor did he escape after supper until he had sung his club song, and had received a somewhat boisterous encore.

Such a custom had it become with the secretary to encounter Wildrake at some point in his walk home between the Loafers' Tavern and Thames Street that he had begun of late actually to miss the companionship of his troublesome charge. The habit of looking out for the old clerk on doorsteps or in dark corners still clung to him; for scarcely a night had passed for many years—until this change in the man's character had developed itself—without the weird figure of Wildrake being discovered by the way. The sense of desolation in Nedlicott's mind became almost as deep as though Wildrake were dead; Thames Street seemed to have grown longer and more dismal through the absence at this solitary and silent hour of the night of the 'bad one' at his side.

Glancing about him—up one dark street and down another—Nedlicott observed, when coming in sight of the approach to Southwark Bridge, some one advancing at a quick pace. Passing under the light of a street lamp, the figure was at once recognisable as Wildrake's. In his hand he carried a heavy stick. His walk was firm and his manner resolute, and his face exhibited the same dogged look of unchangeable purpose which Nedlicott had remarked there when he had last encountered this strange individual.

The secretary stood at the corner of

the street, almost in his path, waiting for him. But Wildrake passed without a sign of recognition—without turning his head to the right or to the left. He was looking pale and haggard, in spite of his apparent energy. His whole appearance was more neglected, his hair whiter, and his eyes wild and vacant in expression, as though that one haunting thought still pursued him which had seemed to predominate so fiercely upon the night on which he had complained to Nedlicott that he had been struck down.

It was impossible for Nedlicott, as he regarded Wildrake, to conceal from himself his sense of increased anxiety at this rapid alteration, and he was forced to agree with the old Jew in giving a preference to Wildrake's state of drunken imbecility as less alarming than his present sullen and incomprehensible condition.

Not being eager at this late hour, and while he was in this strange mood, to attract Wildrake's attention, Nedlicott followed the old clerk as he hurried along Thames Street and entered the court-yard.

Stopping in the shadows at the gateway, Mr. Cheadle's secretary watched him mount the steps under the solitary lamp-light, and let himself into the house without lingering for an instant outside. Never, during all the years that Nedlicott had known Wildrake, had he seen him manifest so much firmness and force of character: and, had Wildrake's face worn a different expression, he would have hailed this transformation with a certain degree of hope for the man's future. But every phase in his conduct pointed towards a tragic end: he had apparently only encountered along his downward course a different current with which he was drifting faster than before.

CHAPTER IV.

A FAMILY QUESTION.

DRESSED for the reception at Lady Mounthaw's, the last reception of the season, Marion descended from her room to join her father in his library.

It was the same library which she had so often entered, when a child, with an awe-stricken face and timid step: a great, solemn-looking room that in those wondering days of childhood had appeared to her to contain a thousand mysteries: the thick, dark-red curtains drawn across the windows concealed behind their massive folds, as she thought, secrets too profound to be divulged; and the huge book-case, which covered the whole of one wall, had perplexed her even more: for she had once seen her father pass through a door in the very centre of it, and disappear from sight. As she stood before her father now, and looked around her, these infant fancies rose vividly in her mind. Nothing in the room was changed: it was a room which seemed to illustrate a memorable page in the earliest records of her life.

Rising from his chair, as soon as Marion appeared, Paul Aldershaw stepped forward to meet her. He had never paid her this attention before: one of which she did not fail to fully comprehend the meaning. It was the first indication her father had given her that he no longer considered her a child.

No frown darkened his brow: there was even something approaching a smile upon his face as he placed his hands gently on Marion's shoulders.

He held her at arm's length to study her appearance.

'Why, Marion,' said he, with a sudden flash of admiration in his eyes, 'I never saw you looking so handsome.'

There is a supreme moment in everyone's life when the last vestige of childhood vanishes. This was Marion's. She was now a woman possessed of worldly cares: and they had come to her as a sad birthright that must be borne. She was indeed more beautiful; for these very cares had given new shades of expression to her face: there was an intenser look in her eyes, a defiant curl about the lips, and a more erect and dignified bearing. All traces of the girl were effaced.

But it had only been by exerting a strong mastery over her inclinations that Marion had gained sufficient strength to control the impulse to rebel against her unhappy destiny; it was then that she recognised the stern need of bending to her father's will. To accept his decision with regard to Roy Valroy was an obvious duty. His life had been clouded for years by a dark and overwhelming sorrow; and she was ready to make any sacrifice which could remove the weight of grief, in some measure, from his heart.

'Sit down, Marion,' said Paul Aldershaw, placing his daughter in his own arm-chair near the fire. 'I wish to say a few words to you before we start for Palace Gardens.'

He took one or two turns across the room at a thoughtful pace. Marion watched him without a word; but her heart was beating painfully with expectation. Then he came and stood beside her, with one arm leaning on the mantel-shelf, and looked down earnestly into her face.

'I am not quite sure,' said he, in a slow, formal tone, ' whether I mentioned to you, Marion, that when you were staying with the Cheadles at Tarmouth Lord Mount-haw dined with me here in a quiet, bachelor fashion. While his son, that excellent young friend of mine, and a few gentlemen I had invited to meet him, were amusing themselves in the billiard-room after dinner, the earl and I had a little chat together over our coffee; quite a friendly little chat,' repeated the merchant prince, pensively, 'and, as you may suppose, Lord Mounthaw made very kind inquiries after you.'

Pausing for a moment, with a keener glance at Marion, he resumed :

'Well, I need not tell you, I am convinced, what an interest the Mounthaw family take in everything connected with your happiness. Lady Mounthaw looks upon you, as Lord Mounthaw remarked on this very occasion, almost in the light of a daughter. She sent you a message— and one which you will appreciate—expressing her regret that she had seen so little of you in town during this season. You will not forget, I know, to assure Lady Mounthaw how much you value such indications of friendship. Did you see much of Lord Dwyver at Tarmouth?'

'Yes,' said Marion, in a low tone, 'he called rather often.'

'Ah,' said her father, drawing himself up in front of the fire, 'I'm glad to hear that. It will please Lady Mounthaw.'

After warming his hands behind his back for a moment, the merchant again regarded his daughter.

'The fact is, Marion,' he pursued, 'we must always bear in mind that the Mounthaws, in Yorkshire, are distinguished neighbours of ours: and,' added Mr. Aldershaw, 'I cannot too strongly impress upon you the importance of im- improving our friendly relations with the family. Is it not clear that the Mounthaws are constantly seeking our society? Lord Dwyver may have had a hundred reasons, as far as I know, for choosing the coast of Tarmouth for his yachting expeditions this year. Tarmouth is considered an excellent little harbour, and most convenient for the regattas; but the fact that he often called at the châlet proves that he has adopted, to a certain extent, his mother's views about you. And you know what they are: no one is to be compared with Marion? Eh?'

'It is very gratifying,' said the girl, distressfully, with her eyes bent to the ground, 'to know that Lady Mounthaw—that anyone—cares for me.'

A slight shadow crossed Paul Aldershaw's face.

'Is that,' said he, 'is that quite the tone, Marion, I have a right to expect?

I must confess I do not understand you.'

Marion, her head still bent, made no reply.

'One would really suppose,' Mr. Aldershaw resumed, 'that you doubted whether these friendly demonstrations on the part of the Mounthaw family were genuine. I am at a loss to conjecture, if such is the case, what your reason can be. Surely Lady Mounthaw could not, with justice, be accused of any want of sincerity in her motive? If her expressions of love for you are not inspired by feelings of pure affection, I am a worse judge of character than I fancied. Ever since you were a child,' persisted the merchant prince, emphatically, 'playing in the grounds about Mounthaw Castle with her son, Lady

Mounthaw has seemed to me to take quite a tender interest in you. It would be strange if, after years of close observation, I should happen to have been deceived; very strange indeed.'

Marion looked up into her father's face.

'I have never,' said she, 'had any reason to question Lady Mounthaw's affection for me.'

'Then what,' demanded Mr. Aldershaw, 'what is it, Marion, that displeases you? From your manner it would seem that my reference to the Mounthaw family is distasteful; and consequently you must not be surprised if I appear somewhat irritated. It grieves me to find that you should think it advisable to take up such an attitude.'

Again the merchant prince began to pace to and fro, glancing sternly at Marion as she had so often seen him look when she was a child.

Paul Aldershaw was naturally mistrustful; and his commercial training had tended to develop this feature in his character. For not only were his suspicions easily roused, but, even in the face of evidence proving that he was unjustified in his conclusions, he would sometimes exhibit an extraordinary bias which no argument would remove.

'It would be too absurd,' said he, stopping suddenly in the centre of the room, ' too absurd to imagine that any conversation you may have had with your cousin, Ada Cheadle, has prejudiced you against any particular member of the Mounthaw family. The Cheadles, though not overrefined, would scarcely be guilty of deriding my friends, the Mounthaws; nor can I believe, even did Mr. Cheadle indulge in any of his vulgar, dramatic insinuations, that my daughter's judgment would be affected. No, Marion; your apparent indifference, when a woman of Lady Mounthaw's disposition shows such an attachment for you, is quite unaccountable.'

Marion rose from her chair, and, with an appealing look, approached her father.

'I cannot bear,' said she, clasping her hands, 'to hear you judge me so harshly. You would not if you only understood me better. I am thankful, from my heart, that I am so fortunate as to have attracted Lady Mounthaw towards me. But what I want, what I desire much more is to gain your love. Did you only know,' added the girl, in a tone of intense fervour, 'how I have longed for years to be devoted to you, to get closer to your heart, you could not misinterpret my meaning as you have done to-night.'

Her face was pale and animated: and, as she ceased to speak, her eyes, kindling with passion, flashed a reproachful glance at her father; but the look soon melted into one of tenderness, through gathering tears.

Silence ensued. Paul Aldershaw's face expressed the struggle at work within him. He turned away impatiently, and stepped towards the hearth, and stood once more with his back to the fire. His head was bent, and his brow became deeply wrinkled and careworn. Suddenly he raised his eyes, and fixed them upon his daughter.

'Marion,' said he, in a subdued tone,

stretching out his hands towards her. 'Marion, my child!'

The girl, uttering a cry of joy, sprang towards her father. He received her in his arms.

'Don't think, my dear,' said he, touching her forehead with his lips, 'don't think any more about the past. All that must be forgotten now. In speaking to you this evening about the Mounthaw family, I had but one object: your future happiness. Lord Mounthaw has spoken to me about his son. He and Lady Mounthaw are anxious to see him settled in life. They have taken me into their confidence: they have frankly acknowledged that ever since you and the young viscount made each other's acquaintance as children, at Mounthaw Castle, they have cherished a hope that you might some day form an attachment. You have, both of you, arrived at a discreet age: so I have promised the earl, as Ada Cheadle may have told you, to ascertain what your sentiments might be about an alliance with the house of Mounthaw.'

At these words, the thoughts of her love for Roy rose up before Marion with crushing force. Her heart was filled with pain and despair; for she knew that it was a hopeless passion—that they had agreed to part, and had parted. But the dream was not ended: it could never end. While she lived, she could give her love to no other man. The mere suggestion that she should marry Lord Dwyver increased her devotion towards Valroy.

Her father waited in silence, as though expecting some reply. But Marion could not trust herself to speak.

'Perhaps,' said Mr. Aldershaw, kindly, 'perhaps you would like to take time for reflection. It were but right. Follow your own inclinations: I have no desire to influence you—to do so would be immoral and unjust. It would give me great pleasure, I admit, to see you the wife of Lord Dwyver: I have wished for years that such an event might come about some day. But I will only say one word more about it now. This offer of marriage— as I think we may almost consider it— is one of the most enviable that could well fall to any woman's lot in life. It would be looked upon by the world as a brilliant match: for two wealthy estates, adjoining each other, in Yorkshire, would eventually belong to one family: the great family of Mounthaw. It would become one of the richest families in the kingdom.

But,' concluded the merchant prince, 'we will talk no more about the matter to-night. It is time we were starting for Palace Gardens. So think it over quietly, Marion. I have no wish to hasten your decision.'

It was nearly midnight when Paul Aldershaw and his daughter drove up to the Earl of Mounthaw's house in Palace Gardens, St. James's. Every approach was blocked with carriages; for a rumour of some political movement was in the wind, and a crush was the natural consequence.

Having ascended the crowded staircase, the merchant prince, with Marion on his arm, had some difficulty in making his way through the ante-room and boudoir, into the drawing-room where Lady Mounthaw was 'seated.' They reached her chair at last.

'I can never forgive you, Miss Aldershaw,' said the countess, 'for your long absence from town, unless you make me a promise.'

Marion smilingly demanded by what means she could reinstate herself in Lady Mounthaw's good graces.

'You must walk over from Oaklands every day this Christmas, and lunch with us at Mounthaw.'

Oaklands was the name of Mr. Aldershaw's estate in Yorkshire.

'It will be a delightful pilgrimage,' said Marion, 'across the park.'

The countess turned laughingly to the merchant prince.

'Could anything, Mr. Aldershaw, be more fair?'

The Countess of Mounthaw had small, delicate features. The paleness of her complexion was remarkable: but what rendered it so strikingly white and transparent in appearance was the almost raven hue of her hair. Her eyes were of a dark blue: they expressed the benignity and brightness of her disposition; for they sparkled whenever she spoke. Homeliness and keen sympathy gave characteristic beauty to her face. But Lady Mounthaw's engaging manner, and her intense vivacity, were her chief attractions in society.

Lord Mounthaw joined them. After exchanging a few words with Marion, he addressed himself to Paul Aldershaw.

'You have heard,' said he, conclusively, 'the latest news from Yorkshire?'

'No.'

'Is it possible? Our member,' said

the earl, 'has accepted the Chiltern Hundreds.'

'The member for Mounthaw?'

'Yes. The Right Honourable gentleman,' replied Lord Mounthaw, with parliamentary playfulness, 'the member for Mounthaw.'

'It is time,' Mr. Aldershaw declared. 'He must be eighty.'

'Seventy-six. He has represented our borough in Parliament for thirty-five years.'

'Is Lord Dwyver on shore,' inquired the merchant, 'and ready to address the constituents?'

'Yes. He is here to-night. To-morrow,' said the earl, 'he starts for Mounthaw.'

The coming election was the principal topic of conversation at Lady Mounthaw's reception. Marion, as she moved with her father among this brilliant gathering, heard scarcely any other subject discussed. In their progress they encountered the embryo member for Mounthaw. In appearance the viscount displayed his accustomed vigorous health and energy. His face was ruddy and sunburnt; for he had just landed from a long cruise, and had brought evidences of the sea-breeze with him to Palace Gardens.

'We got caught off the Needles in a terrific storm,' said he, conversing with Marion, in his emphatic style; 'and, though we were as nearly lost as possible, I never enjoyed myself so much in my life.'

He talked to her of Tarmouth and of the sea. But Marion's thoughts were wandering in other directions, and she could scarcely conceal from Lord Dwyver that what he was saying did not interest her very deeply. She was dreaming of Roy Valroy, and wondering where he was, and whether he was thinking of her. More than once she fancied that she saw his face in the great, changing crowd assembled around her; for Marion knew that Roy was related to the Mounthaw family, and sometimes attended their receptions.

But as she was standing at the head of the staircase, before descending with her father to their carriage, some words reached her ear which completely dissipated all hope of gaining a glimpse of Roy that evening.

The conversation was being carried on between a group of gentlemen standing near Marion.

'Why does not Mr. Valroy contest the borough?'

'He would have no chance: Lord Dwyver is the popular candidate.'

'That may be. But was not Mr. Valroy's grandfather at one time member for Mounthaw?'

'Half a century ago. However, Mr. Valroy has left England.'

'Indeed?'

'Yes. He has gone to Africa to join an exploring expedition. I met his friend, Mr. Ludlaw, at the club. Lord Dwyver will be elected without opposition.'

The words 'left England' sank like a heavy blow upon Marion's heart. Roy Valroy had started upon a journey into a country in which his life would be endangered at every turn. It was all her fault. She had driven him abroad; and if he met his death she would die of grief. A mist gathered before her eyes; the faces around her grew dim, and the sound of voices seemed more distant and subdued. She pressed her father's arm to hasten his steps. He looked at her in alarm, and spoke to her; but she could not answer. She clung more closely to his side, fearing that her senses would forsake her, and that she would fall before they could reach their carriage. A feeling of suffocation almost stifled her as they made their way down the staircase.

Marion was conscious that people moved aside for them to pass, and that her sudden indisposition caused a commotion among Lady Mounthaw's guests. Then she thought she heard among others Lord Dwyver's voice.

She was in the open air at last. It quickly revived her. She looked round, and saw the viscount standing at her side.

'Are you better, Miss Aldershaw?' he inquired, with concern.

Marion thanked him. It was nothing: only a little faintness. She was quite recovered.

The carriage came to the door. Marion stepped in, followed by her father.

'I shall call to-morrow, before leaving town,' said Dwyver, as he stood at the carriage-window. 'My mother will be terribly anxious, Miss Aldershaw, to know how you are.'

'You are very kind,' said the merchant prince. 'Your visit will be very welcome. Good night.'

Not a word passed between Marion and her father during the drive home. They soon reached the great Tyburnian square and drew up at Paul Aldershaw's mansion. In the hall Marion bade her father good-night and hastened to her own room.

She dismissed her maid, and sank down wearily, though with a certain sense of relief at finding herself alone. The events of the evening recurred with cruel force to her mind.

Marion dreaded most thoroughly the prospect of meeting Lord Dwyver on the morrow: and yet if she refused she would incur displeasure. But her confiding nature shrank from the thought of secrecy; she was seized with a resolution to confess to her father that she loved Roy Valroy—that it was a passion too deep to admit of the possibility of ever marrying another. Such an avowal to him might alienate them once more: the estrangement between them might become even greater than when she was a child. Still if she shared the burden of her distress, by so candid a declaration of her unconquerable love, a heavy weight would be removed from her heart.

All these thoughts kept her brain too restless for sleep. She waited with wakeful eyes for the dawn.

CHAPTER V.

THE MICE PLAY.

One Sunday, on a bright December morning, Kate Snowby tripped into Madame Hélène's room dressed for church, in the prettiest of bonnets, and looking as fresh and rosy as though it were a midsummer's day.

'Is Mr. Nedlicott coming this afternoon?' said her friend, looking up with a smile from a bundle of letters which she was reading at her desk.

'We expect him to dinner,' said Katie.

'Father received a letter from Mr. Nedlicott last night.'

'Did he mention anything about . . .' Madame Hélène hesitated, 'Mr. Wildrake?'

'Yes.'

'What has happened?'

'Nothing,' said Kate, 'nothing that need alarm you. He simply repeats, perhaps more emphatically, that no time should be lost in removing him from his present wretched lodging.'

'No time shall be lost,' said Madame Hélène, with firmness. 'I have heard from my lawyer at last. He has appointed to see me to-morrow.'

'I am glad of that,' said the girl, sympathetically, 'for this cruel suspense is making you look terribly ill.'

'It is killing me,' said Madame Hélène,

in a low tone. 'If it had not been for Mr. Nedlicott's kindness I could never have borne it so long. I hope some day to thank him for his friendship towards my poor father.'

'Will you not dine with us to-day?'

'No, Katie. I am not fit company for anyone at present. I must postpone the pleasure a little longer of making Mr. Nedlicott's acquaintance.'

Kate Snowby had begun to look forward, as a natural event, to Nedlicott's visits on Sunday; and her father, had he been as observant in domestic life as he was in commercial, would have remarked that Katie's face grew brighter when the day of rest came round.

Snowby was waiting for his daughter in the hall, with some signs of impatience: for punctuality was part of his religion.

He was a regular attendant at the little church, at the end of the 'boulevard,' with its unfinished steeple and monotonous bell which was now clanging madly in the sharp cold air.

'Been having a gossip, my dear,' said Snowby, ' with Madame Hélène ?'

'She was inquiring about the old clerk.'

'Ah,' said Snowby, with a serious look, ' I'm afraid, from Nedlicott's account, that Wildrake is going from bad to worse. But we shall hear,' he added, 'what he has to report when he comes to-day. No news about that man, however distressing, would surprise me. I look upon him as lost.'

Kate made no reply; and they walked the rest of the way to church in silence. After the service was over, Kate Snowby proposed, as it was such a fine day, that they should take a little stroll before dinner.

'Which way shall we go?' Snowby inquired.

Kate modestly suggested that the road leading to the railway station was a pleasant walk.

'Well, my dear,' said the manager, 'I confess I never saw anything remarkably pleasant about it. But perhaps,' he went on to acknowledge, ' perhaps, as it leads to the City, that may be prejudice on my part. Do you think that Nedlicott will come down by train?'

Katie did not, of course, feel competent to form any opinion upon that question.

'He might, you know,' said Snowby; 'and if we met him, why, we could then return home by the cabbage fields and get an appetite for dinner.'

How pretty Kate Snowby looked—how buoyant and happy! Could her father suppose when he glanced into her face that it was entirely caused by the prospect of a walk through cabbage fields with him? The manager cannot have been so blind as that.

By some extraordinary coincidence, just as they came in sight of Brixton Station, Nedlicott stepped out into the road and advanced towards them.

'Why, father,' said Katie, in a tone of well-feigned surprise, 'there he is!'

A walk round the outer boundaries of a market-garden in a London suburb, on a winter's morning, could scarcely be considered romantic. But there was something in Katie's light step and cheery laugh which seemed to Nedlicott to make both time and place enchanting.

It was a very short walk, far too short in Nedlicott's opinion; and neither he nor Katie had much to say to each other. Indeed, Snowby did most of the talking.

'Well, Nedlicott,' said he, as they strolled along, 'is Mr. Cheadle's comedy a success? By-the-by,' he added, without waiting for a reply, 'it was very thoughtful of you to send us tickets. But we don't, you see, often go to the theatre. It's too far for quiet people like ourselves, too inconvenient. When Mr. Grimwade's room has been dusted—and I have every reason to believe that Mr. Aldershaw is thinking seriously of having it done—we shall take a house in the West-end. And as soon as we get settled down we shall have a carriage. We must pay several visits to the Frivolity then, and have our laugh over Mr. Cheadle's comedies. Mustn't we, Katie?'

'Yes, father,' said Katie, 'if you like.'

'If I like?' Snowby ejaculated.

Katie took her father playfully by the arm, and looking up into his face replied, in a laughing tone:

'Why, you know very well, father, that you could not make me more contented than I am now. So, if we went to live in the West-end, it would be to please you, not to make me happier.'

Snowby glanced at Mr. Cheadle's secretary.

'Now, would you believe it, Nedlicott?' said he. 'That's always the answer my daughter gives me when I talk about a house near Hyde Park and a carriage and pair!'

Having dispensed with all ceremony

towards Nedlicott, on the evening of his first visit to the villa, Snowby offered no apology for dining down-stairs on Sundays in the 'snuggery.' Mr. Aldershaw's manager had long ago explained to the secretary that—the late Mr. Grimwade's office being still in a dusty condition—it was necessary to give as little trouble as possible, as they kept only one servant: in fact, that accumulation of dust in the old City square was made responsible for every difficulty in Snowby's household. As soon as that business of dusting was accomplished, the new leaf would be turned over.

After dinner Snowby produced an excellent bottle of wine and a box of cigars of the best brand: 'samples,' as the manager acknowledged with a wink, 'from friends in the City.'

Katie had gone to have a talk with

Madame Hélène, and the two men were seated over their samples, Snowby discussing their merits in the best commercial style. When the manager's eloquence was fairly exhausted, Nedlicott ventured to broach the subject of Wildrake.

'Is the prospect better,' said Nedlicott, 'of providing a home for Mr. Aldershaw's old clerk?'

Snowby shook his head doubtingly.

'The delay,' said he 'makes me begin to despair. The question still remains: Will any more be done for him than is done at present? But we shall know for certain in a few days.'

For a moment Nedlicott made no reply. Then he said:

'I have no wish, as you know, to pry into other people's affairs. But I would suggest, Mr. Snowby, that those who talk of providing a more congenial lodging for Wildrake should be told that, in a few days, it may be too late.'

'May I ask your reason . . .'

'Yes. It is only right you should know,' said Nedlicott.

He paused, looked pensively at Snowby, and then added:

'Wildrake has met the man who, as he declares, robbed him of his daughter.'

'Is it possible?'

'They encountered each other,' said Nedlicott, 'upon some heath, as far as I can ascertain, near London. Angry words passed between them. Wildrake was struck down. He was left half stunned on the road-side. That is his story. I met him in Fleet Street, on his way home, the very night upon which this happened. He was so altered, I scarcely knew him.'

'For the worse?'

'Yes. So, at least, I consider,' replied Nedlicott, 'although he has given up drinking. He talks no more about his daughter. His whole mind, I am convinced, is bent upon revenge.'

Snowby's face became grave.

'I begin to understand more clearly,' said the manager, 'Mr. Aldershaw's words to me when he asked me to look after Wildrake.'

'What did he say?'

'That a man of Wildrake's habits was a danger to society,' replied Snowby; 'that, if the thing was possible, we must keep him out of mischief.'

'That is my opinion,' said Nedlicott. 'I see in this change cause for great anxiety. It is only in the power of his friends, if he has any, to avert a tragic end.'

For a moment both men were silent. Then Snowby said :

'I will lose no time in consulting Mr. Aldershaw's views on the subject. There is one other, whose name I should not be justified in mentioning, who must not be kept in ignorance of what is happening. Pardon me. I am forced to be somewhat mysterious even in talking about Wildrake with you.'

'Don't let that trouble you,' said Nedlicott.

Meanwhile, Katie, having had her talk with Madame Hélène began to bethink herself of the household duties which, on a Sunday afternoon, fell to her lot : for once a week the servant was allowed a few hours' liberty. The tea table had to be laid in the back parlour, or more strictly speaking in Katie's boudoir; and Kate prided herself on having everything prepared by the time her father had finished his after-dinner cigar in the snuggery.

To Katie's surprise she found, on entering her little boudoir, that Nedlicott was there alone. He was standing at the window looking very thoughtfully across the cabbage-fields at the setting sun.

'Where is father, Mr. Nedlicott?' said she.

'Down-stairs in his arm-chair,' replied Nedlicott, smiling. 'He seemed, I thought, inclined to have a nap. So I left him.'

'He sometimes takes forty winks, as he calls it,' said Katie, 'on Sunday afternoons.'

She began to clear some books from the table, and then took from the cupboard a tea-tray upon which she arranged a small china tea-set which seldom made its appearance except on Sundays, or special occasions.

'You always seem to me so very busy,' said Nedlicott, in a slightly discontented tone, as he watched every movement of the young girl.

'Do I?' said Katie, absently, while arranging the cups and saucers.

'So busy,' Nedlicott continued, 'that we never have any talk together.'

'No?'

'Never,' asserted Nedlicott. 'Yet I have been wishing to say a few words to you for . . . well, I don't know how long. Won't you sit down now?'

Katie gave Nedlicott a swift glance.

'Let me make the tea first,' she pleaded; 'may I?'

'No.'

'I won't be a minute, I promise you. May I, please?'

'No.'

Katie sank into a chair.

'I never thought,' said she, 'that you could be such a tyrant.'

Nedlicott took a seat beside her.

'Do you dislike me for it?'

'N—no.'

'That gives me courage,' Nedlicott declared. 'It is very far from my wish to displease you.'

For a moment he was silent.

'Miss Snowby,' said he, looking tenderly into her face, 'from the first evening I saw you—that delightful evening we passed together in the little room down-stairs—I have longed to tell you what I can now no longer keep to myself. I love you. If you can give me any hope of ever gaining your affection, you will make me happier than I can find words to express.'

Katie bent her head, and made no answer.

'I know very well,' Nedlicott confessed, 'that, in the very short time we have been acquainted, it is unfair to expect that you should look upon me even as a friend. But it seems to me as though I had known you not for a few weeks only, but for years. Indeed, from Sunday to Sunday is like a life-time: for I look forward so eagerly to seeing you again.'

Katie, with her head still bent, said, in a low tone:

'The week seems very long to me.'

'Katie! Is it possible, when I am away, that you sometimes give me a thought?'

'Sometimes!' Katie echoed, with tears in her eyes. 'I am always thinking about you, and all your kindness to that poor old clerk. Do you remember telling us all about him that evening in the snuggery? How he must love you! No one, who knows what a generous heart you have, could help loving you. But I never dreamt,' she added, in a tone of wonder, 'that you cared for me.'

'Darling! I love you with all my heart.'

Katie raised her face. Her eyes beamed with a passion she tried no longer to conceal. The ruby lips, half-parted, seemed to solicit a kiss: and Nedlicott lost no time in snatching the first kiss that a lover had ever placed upon them.

For a while, neither spoke a word. The sun went down beyond the cabbage-fields, and Katie's household duties were left to take care of themselves.

'May I speak to your father, Katie?' Nedlicott presently demanded.

Katie reflected for a moment before replying.

'I think,' said she, with a slight smile, 'that, if I spoke to him myself, perhaps it would be wiser. He has, as you know, rather odd ideas about me. Not that he ever dreams, in his kind heart, of anything beyond my happiness: but he has a pet notion that his daughter ought to make a brilliant marriage in that fashionable circle in which Mr. Aldershaw moves, in the neighbourhood of Tyburnia or Park Lane. He seems to forget how quietly she has been brought up, and what simple tastes she has acquired as his little housekeeper. The fact that Mr. Aldershaw has of late vaguely hinted at a junior partnership in the great house, has rather turned his dear old head. His castles in the air must be very cautiously destroyed. Don't you agree with me?'

'Yes, Katie,' said Nedlicott, 'for I am very far from being rich. I cannot offer you a home such as your father would choose. I can provide nothing larger than a little house like this one.'

'I wish for nothing better,' cried Katie. 'I have told my father a hundred times how contented I am. In a grand London house, I should be wretched. You heard me say so to-day.'

'Yes: and I gathered hope from your words,' said Nedlicott. 'But, Katie, when you speak to your father he will probably exclaim, "Who is Edward Nedlicott? I only know him as Mr. Cheadle's secretary and as a member of the Fresco Club. I should like to know something about his birth and parentage!" We must not forget that.'

'Edward?' said Kate, dreamily. 'What a charming name! But does not Mr. Wildrake always call you Ned?'

'Very often.'

'I thought so,' remarked Katie, in a still more dreamy tone, 'for I always think of you as Ned. May I call you Ned?'

Nedlicott laughed, and smoothed her cheek caressingly.

'Whatever you please, my sweet one.'

'Well, then, Ned,' said Katie, dimpling with smiles. 'Please go on. Your birth and parentage: how like a romance that sounds!'

'Yes: the opening chapter,' said Nedlicott. 'Does it not? I was born, my beloved, of poor but respectable parents. My father, who was a wholesale and retail chemist in the East-end, died when I was a mere child.'

'Is this true?'

'Yes: founded on fact. My mother, anxious to provide a comfortable home for her only son (that's me), purchased a small tobacco business in the neighbourhood of Queenhithe, where she still resides.'

'Wholesale and retail?'

'Retail only. The son (that's me again) occupies the first-floor front: the table in this little room is strewed with prompters' copies of Mr. Cheadle's plays. The library, it should be mentioned, fills a couple of shelves in a remote corner: it is principally composed of Pepys' diary, and odd volumes of the British drama. In an arm-chair, drawn near the fire, this only son has sometimes indulged in wild dreams of one day winning the heart and hand of . . .'

'What nonsense!' cried Katie, laughing. 'But seriously. May I pay your mother a visit soon? I long to see her.'

'Everything depends,' said Nedlicott, 'upon your father.'

'Yes, I know,' said Katie, pensive once more,—'I know.'

'My mother,' Nedlicott declared, 'will be delighted to make your acquaintance: though there is one thing you have done,' added he, with a smile, 'for which you will find it difficult to gain her forgiveness.'

'What can that be?'

'Before I met you,' said Nedlicott, 'I never quitted the house on Sunday. For my absence—every Sunday now—my mother lays the blame at your door.'

Katie looked up earnestly into her lover's face.

'We must not let our happiness give others a moment's pain,' said she. 'I shall go and cheer up the old lady on week-days when you are away. She will forgive me then.'

'She will forgive you to-night,' said Nedlicott, 'as soon as she knows how happy you have made her son.'

Listen! Could that be Snowby's step upon the stairs? Katie jumped up and began to busy herself about making the tea. Fortunately the little brass kettle on the hob was just beginning to boil over: so no more time must be lost. But it really was getting rather too dusky for two young people, not known as lovers, to be found seated alone on a Sunday afternoon. However, Nedlicott, accustomed to 'situations,' had lit the candles and lowered the window-blind before Mr. Aldershaw's manager made his appearance upon the scene.

'Why, Katie,' said he, stepping into the room, 'I think I must have fallen asleep.'

'So I was just saying to Mr. Nedlicott,' replied Katie, emptying tea-spoonfuls of tea into the teapot in a reckless manner. 'Your forty winks have been four hundred to-day. I was thinking seriously of coming downstairs to wake you up.'

The evening seemed to Katie to pass

more quickly than any evening since she had known Nedlicott; for her heart was overflowing with happiness in the knowledge that she was loved. Her light step became lighter, and her laugh more merry still. Even her beauty gained expression. A dreamy look softened at certain moments the scintillations which lit up her eyes, and the dimples, playing about the corners of her mouth, were sometimes subdued by an air of unwonted thoughtfulness. These delicate lights and shades, in Nedlicott's opinion, enhanced her loveliness.

So the hour soon came round for Nedlicott to take his leave, and Katie could scarcely suppress the tears which sprang to her eyes. But her father, offering to walk with their friend to the station, she ran to fetch his hat, and helped him with his over-coat; and in this way she managed to conceal the pang which she felt at parting with her lover for the first time.

Katie stood upon the steps watching them down the 'boulevard' into the darkness. She then closed the door reluctantly, and went upstairs to Madame Hélène.

She was seated near the fire with that look of anxiety which Katie had noticed more frequently of late. The beautiful dark eyes were swollen with weeping, and the brow weary and careworn. But Katie's presence seldom failed to disperse these gloomy shadows; indeed, Madame Hélène called Katie the one ray of sunshine in her life.

'How I envy you, my child,' said she, 'your happy face!'

Katie sank down upon the hearth-rug—her favourite place when alone with Madame Hélène—and, leaning her arms upon the seat of a chair, looked up at her friend.

'Do you remember, Helen,' (this was the name by which Sir Michael Valroy's wife had taught the girl to call her), 'do you remember saying that some day I might know a deeper love than the love I bear towards my father?'

'Yes, Katie, I remember.'

'That love has come to me now,' said Kate; 'a love that I never dreamed of knowing a few weeks ago: a love that I cannot cast out of my heart, even if my father disapproves.'

'He will not oppose your choice.'

'Can you, Helen, guess his name?' said Katie

Helen stroked Kate's head caressingly.

'I guessed it long ago. To-day he has spoken to my Kate.'

'Yes. He has opened his heart to me, and I have given him my love.'

'He has chosen well, Katie,' said Helen, 'and so have you.'

'Oh, I wish that I could think,' said Katie, with a sigh, 'that father will be of your opinion.'

'I have no doubt he will.'

'When he is told that he is not rich?' said Katie; 'and that he doesn't live near Hyde Park?'

'Yes. He will acknowledge him in spite of that.'

Kate became very thoughtful.

'If father does consent,' said she, clasping her hands, 'I shall smother him with kisses.'

Helen regarded the girl with a smile.

'And who, Katie,' said she, 'could wish for a more handsome reward?'

Katie laughed and springing up threw her arms playfully around Helen Valroy's neck. Then, hearing her father's footstep in the hall, she ran down-stairs singing more blithely than any bird on a cloudless morning in spring.

CHAPTER VI.

A COUPLE OF CLIENTS.

ONCE more, after weeks of dreary suspense, Lady Valroy found herself waiting Ludlaw's pleasure in the little prison-like office in Pump Court. There was nothing in the barrister's letter which had brought her there to increase her hope or despair: for it contained no reference to the subject so near to her heart. The day and the precise hour upon which Ludlaw could grant her an interview were specified in polite terms: not a word more. The barrister was not the man to commit himself in writing to any opinion that would leave room for the slightest misinterpretation. He used the law for self-protection with the same skill with which an able soldier wields his sword.

Helen Valroy—for such was Madame Hélène's true name—had hastened to keep the appointment at the hour appointed. Her patience, tried by this long delay, was completely exhausted: and had she not been well acquainted with the characters of the men with whom she was dealing, she would have put her threat to visit John Wildrake into execution after her last interview with Ludlaw. But a certain indefinable dread of the consequences had restrained her. Ludlaw, as Helen had reflected, was a man whom it would be wiser not to offend, and the terror which Sir Michael Valroy had inspired years ago was still something more than a mere recollection. Yet events had begun to assume such a serious aspect that, had Ludlaw allowed another day to expire, she would, in spite of these circumstances, have acted upon her own responsibility. Could Ludlaw be cognisant of this?

It was a question which Lady Valroy asked herself repeatedly. But to get an insight into Ludlaw's mind was as difficult as to gain a glimpse of the outer world between the bars of the dusty window of the room in which she was seated. The lawyer, she well knew, prided himself upon being impenetrable.

The most gloomy thoughts took possession of Helen's mind as the minutes passed without Ludlaw exhibiting any indications of being at leisure. Was he purposely inflicting this additional torture? It was surely cruel enough to have kept her for weeks in a feverish state of anxiety. She felt a strong disposition to escape from this dismal little dungeon, and make good her retreat before her intention could be suspected.

Nearly an hour went by. Had Ludlaw forgotten his appointment? Tired of waiting, and indignant at the lawyer's want of courtesy towards her, Helen Valroy had placed her hand upon the latch, with the intention of leaving the chambers, when a loud knock at the door of the common staircase obliged her to draw back. There was something in the sound familiar to her ears. She stood quite motionless and listened.

She heard the quick step of the office-boy, and the opening of the outer door.

Then an imperious voice demanded: 'Is Mr. Ludlaw at home?'

Helen started.

Sir Michael Valroy!

She sank into the chair, trembling.

'This way, sir, if you please.'

Helen sprang up, with her hand upon the door, as though to prevent his entrance; but, to her relief, the step passed down the passage, another door was opened and shut, and all was silent—all but her heart, which beat fast and loud.

What could this mean? She had been inveigled into a trap. Ludlaw and her husband had plotted together and arranged that the latter should be present at the interview. For a moment all her courage fled—all hope of success forsook her.

But she quickly controlled the overwhelming sense of despair into which the shock from this surprise had thrown her. She recollected the pitiable errand upon which she had come: to demand the right to save her father from the depths of misery, perhaps even from death. Her courage revived; it was better, perhaps, however painful after so many years of separation, that she should meet her husband once more. If she failed to rouse his pity more than she could have done through the mediation of his legal friend, she would at least give a convincing proof that she was sincere in her appeal.

She was scarcely allowed time for these reflections, or to recover her presence of mind, when the boy came to her with the request that she would step into Mr. Ludlaw's room.

Upon the hearth-rug, with his back to the fire, stood Sir Michael Valroy, stroking his dark beard. He glanced sternly at his wife, without any other sign of recognition. Ludlaw, however, rose as she entered, and indicated a chair near his desk. He then resumed his seat between his two clients. Playing with a paper-knife, with which he frequently tapped the palm of his hand, the barrister looked from one to the other with his usual air of abstraction.

'A question has arisen,' said he, glancing at a document lying open upon the desk, 'a question has arisen with regard to a clause in an agreement. This agreement is signed by both of you, and dated prior to your marriage'—he looked from one client to the other, and then more searchingly at the document—' prior to the marriage of Helen Wildrake and Sir Michael Valroy. In a clause, it is stipulated that you, Lady Valroy, should not only cease to hold communication with your father, but guard the fact of your union with Sir Michael Valroy as a secret until such time as your husband might choose to give publicity to the marriage. You do not deny, madame, being a party to this deed?'

'No. There was a clause, as you describe it——'

'One moment! That having been admitted,' said Ludlaw, 'would you kindly state, as a mere matter of form, whether your application to me to obtain from Sir Michael Valroy a certain modification, more especially regarding this clause, was or was not spontaneous?'

Helen Valroy looked from Ludlaw to the baronet with a rapid flash of the eyes.

'I was prompted by my own conscience,' she answered, in a low tone.

'Not by me,' questioned Ludlaw, 'not by any human being?'

'By no living soul.'

Ludlaw regarded Sir Michael shrewdly. At the same time he gave the palm of his hand four distinct taps with the paper-knife, as though mentally and with emphasis repeating Lady Valroy's last words.

'Will you have the goodness,' said Sir Michael, frowning at Ludlaw, and then at his watch, 'to get on a little quicker.'

Ludlaw regarded the baronet with a provoking smile.

'My dear Sir Michael,' said he, 'let me beg of you not to prejudice the case by signs of impatience or ill-temper. You should know, considering how many years we have been acquainted, that my pace is the one at which to arrive most expeditiously at an understanding.'

The lawyer then turned to his other client.

'You had, as I gathered from our last interview,' said he, 'acquired, on your arrival in London, some very distressing intelligence about your father?'

'Yes: from my landlord,' said Helen.

'This landlord being,' Ludlaw prompted her, 'head-clerk in a certain merchant's office, in which John Wildrake had formerly been employed?'

'Yes.'

'Another question,' said Ludlaw. 'Was your father dismissed from this office?'

'Yes.'

'On account of his intemperate habits?'

'So I was told.'

The barrister leaned back in his chair.

'Now,' said he, 'this is precisely, in conveying your message to Sir Michael Valroy, what I stated: that this was the painful news which had reached your ears. John Wildrake had lost his situation, owing to inebriety: moreover, that he was living in a garret, and in a destitute condition. Correct me, if I am wrong.'

He paused, with a look at Lady Valroy. She remained silent with her head bent.

'This being the case,' Ludlaw continued, 'I explained to Sir Michael that you had been moved to compassion—that your sense of duty towards your parent had impelled you to make this request. Your earnest wish was that this clause in the agreement, prohibiting the publicity of your marriage, should be annulled.'

Helen Valroy looked up into Ludlaw's face.

'Not absolutely for my sake,' said she, 'but, because my father vowed not to recognise me as his daughter unless I gave him a convincing proof that I was married. Having gained his forgiveness for my thoughtless conduct, I would, as I assured you, exact from him a promise never to mention my alliance with Sir Michael Valroy.'

The baronet made an impatient movement as though about to speak.

'Permit me!' said Ludlaw, raising his paper-knife expressively. 'That is precisely the point, Lady Valroy, at which we stumble. Sir Michael has no confidence . . . .'

'Never had an atom,' interposed the baronet.

'Never had one atom of confidence,' repeated Ludlaw, 'in John Wildrake: not the man, he considers, to be trusted with a secret. His intemperance, his tendency to gossip with every stray acquaintance he meets with at low taverns, may be cited in support of that opinion. Sir Michael Valroy cannot, under these circumstances, consent to cancel the clause now under consideration in this agreement. Quite impossible!' and Ludlaw struck with the paper-knife the palm of his hand twice, with a pause between each tap, to strengthen the emphasis.

Stroking his beard with an air of satisfaction, the baronet nodded as a sign of approval at the manner in which the lawyer had given utterance to this decision.

For some moments no one spoke. Ludlaw regarded one client and then the other without moving his neck, but with a restless eye. Lady Valroy was the first to break the silence.

'Do me the favour, Mr. Ludlaw,' said she, 'to ask Sir Michael Valroy if he seriously considers that his reason for standing in the way of a reconciliation between me and my father is a sufficient one, considering the very exceptional circumstances of the case.'

Ludlaw looked inquiringly at the baronet.

'Tell Lady Valroy,' said Sir Michael, addressing his legal friend, 'that I consider my reason more than a sufficient one: that if I had been anxious that my name should form a topic of conversation in low taverns I should not have made this binding compact between us. I never believed in Wildrake's sobriety, even in the first days of our acquaintance. There was every need, as events have proved, for taking this precaution.'

The lawyer communicated this reply by a glance at Lady Valroy.

'Does Sir Michael Valroy suppose,' Helen hastened to demand, ' that, having once satisfied my father that I was married immediately after leaving his house, I should not use every means in my power, as I have declared, to enforce the strictest silence? I have formed my plans. If necessary I would even consent to go abroad with my father and never leave him as long as I lived. I am culpable. In acting as I have done, I have brought this misery upon him. I will now devote myself to him gladly—not only as a duty, but with the hope of convincing him that I regret more than I can express the mad step I was persuaded to take without consulting his wishes. Sir Michael Valroy shall never again hear of his unhappy wife—nor of John Wildrake—if he will release her from this promise given fifteen years ago without reflection, without realizing what a cruel wrong she was inflicting upon others.'

With clasped hands, and in a low, supplicating voice, Helen Valroy bending towards Ludlaw's desk made this earnest appeal. Her lips trembled, and tears started to her eyes before she had ceased to speak.

Ludlaw was not unmoved: for he frowned very severely at his paper-knife which he twisted about with his fingers in a rapid, nervous manner.

Sir Michael Valroy showed no sign of emotion.

'Ludlaw,' said he, impatiently, 'is there

any object in prolonging this discussion? I came here to-day at your suggestion. You seem to be of opinion that if I expressed my disapproval, in your presence, there would be no need to remonstrate further with Lady Valroy. This scheme,' he added, in a tone of contempt, 'for conducting John Wildrake into retirement is not worth arguing about. Whether he would, or would not, consent to leave his garret is a matter of pure speculation. At no moment since that deed was signed'— and the baronet pointed to the document on Ludlaw's table—'have I felt less disposed to see it cancelled. I have good reason to suspect, as Lady Valroy may as well know, that John Wildrake is mad. That decides the matter. We are wasting time by listening to all this sentiment. Be kind enough, Ludlaw, to wish Lady Valroy good-morning; and allow me to take my leave.'

Saying which, Sir Michael seized his hat, and stepped towards the door.

'Stay,' said Lady Valroy, rising from her chair and turning towards the baronet. 'I have one question to ask you, Sir Michael, which you cannot refuse to answer. Have you met my father since your return to England?'

Sir Michael stopped and stared fixedly at Lady Valroy.

'Why?'

Helen glanced at Ludlaw and then again faced Sir Michael Valroy.

'Because,' said she, in a broken voice, 'something has reached my ear which I can scarcely credit. I am told that, not many days ago, my poor father encountered you upon Batswing Heath and demanded news of his daughter.'

'What then?'

'I am told,' continued Lady Valroy, 'that you struck him a heavy blow with your fist, and left him lying half-stunned by the roadside.'

'Well?'

'I wish to know if this is true.'

'That I was accosted one night after dark,' said the baronet, defiantly, 'by a maniac, who represented himself to be John Wildrake, is true enough. He stood in my path and used insulting language. I treated him as I should have treated any other tramp. I knocked him down.

Helen Valroy shuddered, and a look of deep pain crossed her face. But she quickly recovered herself, and her eyes flashed with passion:

'You have acted,' cried she, 'not only like a coward, but with a want of foresight which I could hardly have imagined possible in a man of your cunning and calculating nature. I loved you once; and, but for this unpardonable insult to my father, I should have loved you still, in spite of all the heartless treatment I have received. But now I despise and hate you.'

The baronet could not meet her glance. Her scornful tone and her look of anger seemed to cow him. But his face was dark with rage.

'I refused,' continued Lady Valroy, 'to believe this story unless confirmed by Mr. Ludlaw or by you. And if you had agreed to cancel this document, which I was brainless enough to sign, I would never have mentioned the subject. You have forced me to speak by withholding your consent. I must see my father now.'

'Must, Lady Valroy?' questioned Ludlaw.'

'Yes. It is imperative,' she replied, 'that I should see him, and at once.'

'May I ask your reason?' Ludlaw demanded.

'To prevent a crime,' answered Lady Valroy, in a low tone.

'What!' Sir Michael exclaimed, taking a quick step towards his wife.

'Ever since that night,' she replied, 'my father, I am told, has strangely altered. He no longer frequents the taverns at which he was so often seen. All day he remains at home, and after dark he disappears, mysteriously, from the house in Gable Court. His manner, they say, is stern and revengeful. Is it not more than probable that he goes to Batswing Heath, hoping to encounter Sir Michael Valroy? I dread the very thought of another meeting between them. I claim the right, after what has happened, to see my father with a view of pacifying him. It is the least I can do in order to prevent . . .'

The baronet clenched his hand.

'So,' he cried, 'my life is threatened—is it? Ludlaw,' he added, 'what clever trick is this? A likely way of gaining my consent! Let me advise you,'—Sir Michael turned fiercely towards his wife,—'let me advise you to be careful how you play with me!'

He stepped so close to her, with his

clenched hand raised menacingly, that she recoiled with a look of alarm.

Ludlaw rose from his chair.

'Sir Michael!' said he, pursuasively, 'let me implore you to curb your anger. There may be some reason after all for Lady Valroy's anxiety.'

'Nothing of the sort!' retorted the baronet, white with passion. 'I tell you the whole business is a fraud. This woman has come to London on purpose to contrive, if she can, my ruin and disgrace. She has taken lodgings, as she boldly tells us, in the house of Paul Aldershaw's head clerk. What can have been her motive? There can only have been one. It was to spy and plot with John Wildrake's friends until they had revived the fellow's enmity and to direct it against me.'

'Your suspicion,' said Helen Valroy,

with flashing eyes, 'is unjust; it is unmanly. Your name, whatever happened, never escaped by lips. I have considered you, as Mr. Ludlaw knows, from first to last. I have waited for weeks, although hearing the most agonising accounts about my father, because I would not break my promise to you. I have shown some impatience, I will not deny, in my letters to Mr. Ludlaw. But I have done nothing to deserve such a cruel censure as this.'

Ludlaw's face was thoughtful. After a moment's reflection, he turned to Sir Michael and said:

'Lady Valroy is right.'

The only effect of this verdict was to increase the baronet's rage.

'I deny it!' he exclaimed. 'If Lady Valroy was sincere, she would have come forward with this petition years ago. Is it not obvious? Why, surely there can be no question about that! But no—she bided her time, she waited my return from abroad. She thought, by letting this miserable hound loose upon me, to get everything her own way. Does the woman forget with whom she has to deal?'

While speaking, Sir Michael Valroy paced to and fro with quick strides, utterly regardless of the bundles of papers which lay, according to Ludlaw's system of order, upon the floor. He stamped down upon these documents in his anger, or sent one or two flying with his foot across the room at every step.

Ludlaw looked on, speechless with dismay. Suddenly the baronet stopped, in the midst of the scattered documents, and faced his wife with a look of fury in his eyes.

'Let me hear no more,' he warned her, 'about this scandalous affair. Be careful not to act contrary to my decision. You signed the deed without a murmur; you cannot revoke now. It is too late. Make the attempt even by one imprudent word at your peril!'

With these words he went out, treading heavily along the passage, and slamming the staircase-door loudly behind him.

CHAPTER VII.

NOT WISELY, BUT TOO WELL.

MARION entered the breakfast-room on the morning after the reception at Lady Mounthaw's with some degree of trepidation: for she was resolved to confess to her father all that had passed between her and Roy Valroy. The avowal would destroy all the hopes which he had so long entertained of an alliance with the Mounthaw family; and she anticipated a display of indignation which it would be difficult to endure. This reflection, however, did not weaken her in her purpose. The ordeal, as she reasoned, must be gone through, sooner or later. It was better faced at once; she dreaded to think that, by a day's delay, she might be compelled, against her will, to marry Lord Dwyver.

It was late that morning—much later than usual—before Paul Aldershaw made his appearance. He so seldom went into society, beyond an occasional and sedate dinner-party, that even a reception fatigued him. But he came down at last, and without the shadow of a frown upon his brow.

'Marion,' he demanded, glancing out of window, 'what do you say to a drive to the City with me this morning?'

He had never before asked her to accompany him to his office. The girl could hardly believe her senses. For years past she had watched him each morning from her window as he stepped into his carriage, and she had often longed to take a seat at his side. Her eyes sparkled at the prospect of such a new delight.

The merchant remarked the change in her face. He placed his hand gently upon Marion's shoulder.

'No one knows,' said he, 'how tedious this drive is every day—how wearisome city life is to me.'

There was a pensive look in his eyes and a strange sadness in his tone which Marion had never observed before. She glanced up with a timid expression into his face.

'Why do you work so hard,' the girl inquired, 'at what is distasteful? There can be no compulsion where there is so much wealth.'

Paul Aldershaw's brow became clouded.

'Some men are forced to work,' said he, 'even when rich, in order to divert their thoughts. Without incessant occupation, life for years past would have been unbearable.'

He paced once or twice up and down the room in silence. Then, turning towards the door, he beckoned with a solemn uplifted finger to his daughter.

'Come with me to the library. I have something to tell you, Marion.'

He led the way. But, having reached the library, he only paused a moment. Taking a key from his desk, he opened the secret door in the centre of the bookcase—the door by which Marion had seen him disappear so mysteriously when she was a child. He passed through and invited her to follow.

Marion found herself almost in darkness. But her father, stepping forward, drew back some heavy curtains and admitted a flood of light.

They stood in a large room which in every detail resembled an artist's studio. The furniture was antique in character; a great arm-chair covered with green velvet, another of dark wood fantastically carved, rugs lying here and there on the oaken floor, and huge picture-frames leaning against the panelled walls. A small marble statue of Apollo on a pedestal occupied one corner, and many other works of art lay about on the mantelshelf, or on brackets, or on the ground. An easel, near the window, was hidden under massive folds of thick black drapery. The merchant walked towards this easel. Marion watched his movement with a quick beating heart. He glanced at her keenly, and then, with a trembling hand, he lifted the covering and disclosed to view a large picture on the point of completion.

Marion gave an exclamation of surprise. On a low couch lay a child three or four years of age, with fair curling hair and laughing features. Bending over it, in an attitude of devotion, was the figure of a very beautiful woman. Her hands were clasped, and she was gazing at the child with dark passionate eyes, and with a breathless expression upon the half-parted lips. The brow was slightly troubled, as though by some passing thought; otherwise the whole form, as well as the face, indicated a strange and almost painful devotion.

'My mother!'

In a low, awe-stricken voice, Marion uttered the cry, and then, sinking down before the picture, she burst into tears. All the distressing recollections of her lonely childhood recurred as she looked once more upon the face of the one being by whom she had imagined she was loved —the friend that had brightened her day-dreams, and whom she thought that nothing but death could have taken from her.

'Yes,' said the merchant, in a broken voice, 'that is your mother, as I painted her years ago. I worshipped her. I would not have believed it possible that a woman with such a face could be so false to husband and child. I have been cruelly deceived.'

Marion did not speak or move. She still knelt before that faithless mother.

Her tears flowed faster at her father's words.

'Never,' continued he, 'never, Marion, since the day she left us have I touched that picture. I closed my studio. I cursed her, and I cursed the name of Valroy!'

An acute pain passed through Marion's heart. She sprang up; and with a supplicating look she placed her hand upon her father's arm.

'If you cannot forget the past,' said she, 'if you cannot forgive, do not speak a word, I implore you, against the name of Valroy. I cannot bear it! I know that you have every reason to be embittered: I grieve to think of all the agony you must have suffered. I remember my mother bending over me when a child: I have pictured her to myself as you have painted her there. Could you suppose, young as I was, that her loss caused me no sorrow? It has been a sadness for both of us. But it is more than sad, more than piteous now. Can you not guess why I cannot bear to hear you speak against the name? It is the name I love—this name which you have cursed.'

'Marion!'

'I love Roy Valroy—the brother of the man who has brought all this trouble upon our house.'

A look of calm despair, more painful to witness than a burst of anger, came over the merchant's face.

'This,' said he—'this is what I feared.'

Marion regarded her father with deep contrition.

'I cannot change my nature,' she pleaded, with a soft look in her eyes. 'I have tried so hard to forget him! But it is not possible. I shall love him always now—always: as long as I live.'

The merchant knit his brow and demanded, as though uttering his thoughts aloud rather than addressing Marion:

'So he has dared to speak to you of love.'

'Yes. He has spoken.'

'What has been your answer?'

Marion was silent. She stood with her eyes bent to the ground, her long lashes trembling and her lips pale.

'If you have accepted him,' said the merchant, sternly, 'you have ceased to be my daughter. It is a question of choice between him and me.'

'I have chosen.'

She sank down into a chair, in a dreamy

posture, with her head resting on her hand. After a moment's pause, she raised her eyes full of pensiveness.

'When we first met,' said she, in a low tone, 'I did not even know his name: and even if I had I could not have understood that it was wrong to care for him. I was never told to avoid his society: no one warned me, until it was too late, that the acquaintance would incur your displeasure. But when Ada spoke to me, when I understood all, I refused to see him. Only once since then, by mere chance, he found me at the Cheadles' house. And then . . .'

'Well, Marion. What then?'

'We took leave of each other,' continued Marion, tearfully; 'we agreed never to meet any more. I told Roy Valroy that it was your wish and that it was my duty to obey. He owned that he had acted wrongly; and in his disappointment and despair he has gone abroad. He does not intend to return to England: so all is at an end between us.'

'I heard nothing about that.'

'It happened days ago,' said Marion; 'and now,' she added, persuasively, 'can you not understand how impossible it is for me ever to love another? I am willing to do all in my power to please you. But could that be by giving my hand to anyone, however rich or poor, unless I could give with it my whole heart?'

For a moment the merchant made no reply. He stood, lost in thought, with his eyes turned upon Marion.

'I had begun to hope,' said he, 'that this wearisome City life—the wealth that had been added to the house by my unceasing labours—would carry with it some recompense after all. My expectations with regard to an alliance with the Mounthaw family had begun to revive: the dream of my life, that Oaklands and Mounthaw should become one estate, seemed actually on the point of being fulfilled. I am deeply disappointed. Not,' he hastened to add, ' that I blame you. I blame the Cheadles. What right had they to introduce such a character to my daughter?'

'If you only knew how good and noble Roy Valroy is,' said Marion, with spirit. 'If you had met him, you would not deny that. But you never will.'

He placed his hand upon the cloth, and flung it angrily over the picture of his wife and child.

'Those two men,' said he, 'who have, one after the other, brought so many troubles into our lives, must be forgotten:

or, if that be impossible, never mentioned between us. I appreciate your conduct. You have acted honourably in a very difficult and painful affair: I shall never forget that. You have done what was right: you have considered me. You have had the good sense to know that the mere rumour of an alliance, with such a disreputable family, would not only distress me beyond measure, but injure my character and position. You are a loyal daughter.'

The girl rose and stood beside her father, with her head bent, silent and submissive. He kissed her, and with more tenderness than on the previous evening when she had confessed a craving to get nearer to his heart.

'Marion,' said he, in a kindly tone, 'you have given me a strong proof of your affection. If your inclinations are not free ....'

'Indeed, they are not.'

'Why, then, we must mention to the Earl of Mounthaw that for the present ....'

'I shall never change,' said Marion. 'I never can consent to what has been proposed by Lord Mounthaw.'

'Perhaps,' the merchant gently urged, 'in a year, or two years' time ....'

'Never,' said Marion, in a low voice. 'Never.'

'Very well,' he replied, with a suppressed sigh. 'Let us say no more about it. I will write to Lord Mounthaw. That will end the matter.'

As they drove to the City that morning, side by side, Marion knew that she had awakened that latent affection which had lain dormant ever since her father had felt that crushing sorrow. The deep affection had been roused at last. And yet with all the happiness it brought there was one sad reflection which could not be banished. The nearer they were drawn towards each other, the greater became the distance separating her from Roy Valroy. How gladly would she—had such a choice been possible—have offered her life as a preferable sacrifice!

Before descending from his carriage, at the entrance to the old City square, the merchant proposed to Marion that she should drive to Cheyne Walk and spend the day with Ada Cheadle.

'Of course,' said Mr. Aldershaw, 'supposing Lord Dwyver called, you could not receive him. I should not wish it now, even if Miss Blessitt was in town.'

The ex-governess had gone to Oaklands to superintend certain preparations for the reception of the family at Christmas.

'But,' added the merchant, 'my letter to the Earl of Mounthaw makes it very improbable that Lord Dwyver will call. I have written, and I have expressed our decision in terms too distinct to be misinterpreted.'

Frequently during that day, in the midst of his City affairs, Paul Aldershaw rose from his desk and paced to and fro in his office with a restless step. The morning with Marion in his deserted studio and the sight of that painting which he had left unfinished had stirred up stern reflections about the past. The declaration, from his daughter's own lips, that she loved the brother of the man whose very name sent the hot blood tingling through his veins, was intolerable. He would sooner have seen her dead than such a thing should have happened. He reproached himself severely. If he had shown a stronger interest in Marion—if he had not kept her so long in ignorance about her mother—this event would never have occurred: she would never have loved Roy Valroy. But he had not realized, so immersed had he been in his own affairs, that it was possible that anyone, unless it were Lord Dwyver, would win Marion's heart. Too late he had discovered his error—too late he had tried to rectify his fault. For this shortsightedness he was experiencing keen disappointment and deep regret.

Marion's candid avowal of a passion which she had abandoned for his sake, went straight to the merchant's heart. He felt his position painfully. It seemed unjust to deny anything to such a daughter: and if he could have purchased happiness for her at any other price there would have been no refusal, whether the demand were upon his pride or his pocket. But to give his consent to Marion's marriage with a Valroy was impossible: the very thought appeared repulsive to his haughty nature.

His resentment towards Sir Michael Valroy recurred with redoubled force. He was the cause of all the trouble which had overtaken—which had embittered his whole life: and once more he cursed him, as he had cursed him in a moment of supreme agony years ago.

The afternoon shadows gathering in the old square, Paul Aldershaw's lamp was lighted, and his blinds drawn down. Then he began to apply himself to work with strange energy: not like a man who is compelled, through stress of time, to accomplish certain undertakings, but like one who believes by force of work and will to conquer embarrassing thoughts. The struggle was fierce. Watching his face, one would have almost imagined that phantom voices were whispering in his ears. He frequently started, looked wrathfully around the room, and sometimes rose from his chair with his hand outstretched, as if to ward something from him which was getting too near, and even impeding respiration. Pacing once or twice up and down the room, after such an interruption, he settled down again in his chair and began to exert a new impulse for work among his papers. But the maddening voices seemed soon to swarm as before, like irritating insects on a hot summer night. Then, as before, he became enraged and restless. He was as cruelly tormented in his mind as though a fever had attacked his brain.

Suddenly he observed, in one of his pacings, that the door which communicated with the late Mr. Grimwade's room stood open. The discovery startled him: not that there was anything very startling in the fact. For the old ledgers being kept there, besides endless boxes of old letters, which had sometimes to be examined by clerks; and the door, not being easy to close, might have swung open of its own accord. The merchant stepped towards the door, and peered into the dusty old office.

The room was full of murky moonlight; for it entered through grimy panes into this abandoned and sepulchral apartment where the dust lay thick in many places: on the late Mr. Grimwade's desk, on the boxes which lumbered the high shelves, on the cobwebs in corners where flies, as long dead as Mr. Grimwade himself, still clung persistently, as though waiting upon that treacherous field of battle for interment after their unequal fight. The blinds were broken: and, glancing out of window, Paul Aldershaw perceived the crescent moon hanging in a clear wintry sky above the quaint roofs and chimneys of the old houses opposite. The sight seemed to have a chilling effect upon his nerves, for he turned away with a shudder, and, shutting the door, he returned to his chair. His face was still pale and anxious.

He presently took from his drawer a small volume. It was bound with a steel clasp, and was under lock and key. He unlocked the clasp and opened the book. It was a journal, already half-filled with memoranda. With a trembling hand the merchant turned to a page upon which he read his last entry:

'*If John Wildrake murders Sir Michael Valroy, the fault will be mine. It is only by the strictest supervision that the crime may be averted. I can read this terrible fact in Wildrake's face, while he stands before me to-day and throws the blame upon that man's shoulders of his daughter's loss and of his own demoralisation.'*

CHAPTER VIII.

THE DARK POOL.

Upon the same evening, and about the same hour that Paul Aldershaw had looked through the open door into the late Mr. Grimwade's moonlit office, the crescent moon was shining brightly over Batswing Heath. Along a pathway, between the low gorse, came Spicer, the landlord of the 'Hunted Stag,' walking at a brisk pace. The air was bleak, although there was scarcely a breath of wind on the common.

Dressed in a well-fitting top-coat, which

reached below his knees, and a low-crowned hat, Spicer had a very sporting appearance. He had been visiting a neighbour, and was on his way home to supper. He whistled as he went, as innkeepers have an idle knack of doing, in a low tone but with marked vivacity: it is possible that the clear, moonlit sky inspired this musical turn of mind.

Suddenly he stopped whistling. Upon the road, which crossed his path at right angles, he noticed the figure of a man approaching. There was something in the movement and slouching gait which he seemed to recognise. A clump of old trees stood near the high-road. Spicer quickened his pace, and, reaching these trees, concealed himself behind one of them and waited.

The man went by with a hurried step. He passed so near that, by reaching out his arm, Spicer could have touched him. He appeared breathless from running, or from fright: for he coughed and choked, while looking with scared eyes over his shoulder, as he hastened on. His face was deadly pale. His clothes were torn and covered with mud.

Spicer knew him at once: it was Wildrake. It was the man whom Sir Michael Valroy's friend, Ludlaw, had declared he had reason to suspect. The landlord gave vent to a low whistle: but this time the tone expressed intense surprise. Next moment Spicer sprang into the road.

His first thought was to stop Wildrake. But after looking up and down the highway, and neither seeing nor hearing anyone, as he expected he should, in pursuit, he resolved not to interfere. What business was it of his? He was not a constable, and therefore had no authority to arrest a fugitive tramp, or whatever Wildrake might be, on suspicion. It was an affair, to all appearance, for the police. His duty, no doubt, would be to report what he had witnessed. But he did not consider himself justified in taking a personal responsibility in the matter.

With these reflections, Spicer continued on his way towards the 'Hunted Stag.' But Wildrake's face and his strange appearance never ceased to haunt him.

As he stepped into the inn, Spicer looked about him as though half-expecting to see Wildrake seated in the bar-parlour. But the room was empty.

A buxom woman came out of the kitchen to meet the landlord.

'Why, Spicer,' said she, with a glance at his face, ' you look worried.'

Spicer walked into the kitchen and sat down.

'Something has given me a turn.'

The landlady—for it was Spicer's wife—regarded him fixedly.

'Not a ghost, I hope?'

'No; but a man with a face as white, if not whiter.'

'What man?'

Spicer related the incident to his wife. When he had finished, she uttered no comment; but she appeared, nevertheless, to be brooding while she laid the table for supper.

When they had finished their evening meal, and Spicer had lit his pipe, she ventured to make a suggestion.

'I think, Spicer,' said she, 'I'd close

no time, if I were you, in seeing Mr. Ludlaw.'

'What—go to London to-night?'

'He's at Sir Michael Valroy's,' said the landlady. 'I saw him pass by here this evening.'

Spicer jumped up hurriedly.

'Why,' he demanded, tugging on his top-coat, 'why didn't you say so before?'

'Because, Spicer, I didn't wish to spoil your supper.'

Spicer placed his hands on his wife's broad shoulders, and saluted her on each of her plump cheeks.

'My dear,' said he, regarding her with admiration, 'I've always held that you were a woman . . .'

'Hadn't you better start?'

'I'm off!' said Spicer.

Once more the landlord stepped out

quickly across the heath, but with no apparent inclination for whistling now; nor did he seem interested in the splendid moonlight, except so far as it might aid him in choosing the shortest direction towards Sir Michael Valroy's house. Roused to a sense of responsibility at last, Spicer became surprisingly engrossed and energetic. Wildrake's face had inspired in him a grim surmise.

While the landlord of the 'Hunted Stag' was making his way across the heath on his errand to Ludlaw, the barrister was seated in Sir Michael Valroy's dining-room, as he had so often sat before, ensconced in a great arm-chair in front of the fire. His handkerchief as usual was thrown over his face, and he was fast asleep; and as usual the portraits of the Valroy family looked down upon him gloomily out of their frames. Sir Michael had gone, in spite of Ludlaw's protestations, for his walk upon the common. The baronet had been even more restless and perverse since the meeting with his wife in Ludlaw's chambers: his mental condition had, in fact, perplexed Ludlaw. No further conversation on the subject of Lady Valroy's petition, as Ludlaw soon found, was at all possible. At the mere mention of that affair, Sir Michael had flown into a passion more violent than he had exhibited on previous occasions. Ludlaw had therefore been compelled to regard the matter as one which could only be adjusted by time and circumstance.

Ludlaw was awakened by the entrance of a servant. He lifted the handkerchief from his face.

'Spicer has called, sir, and wishes to see you.'

'The landlord of the "Hunted Stag"?'

'Yes, sir.'

'Show him in.'

Spicer stepped softly into the room, hat in hand. He bowed respectfully, seeming to include the portrait of his late master, the old baronet, in his salute.

'Well, Spicer, what's the news?'

'Bad, sir, I'm afraid.'

'Sit down,' said Ludlaw.

The landlord took a seat near the door.

'Well, Spicer?'

'Well, sir,' he replied, 'I've come over, as I thought, in duty bound, to speak to you about a man you may remember seeing one night in the bar-parlour—a man about whom you said you had suspicions.'

'I recollect,' Ludlaw declared. 'A fellow called Wildrake.'

'Yes, that was his name.'

'What about him?'

'I've seen him again this evening.'

'At your inn?'

'No; on the common,' said Spicer. 'He was stepping out at a great rate, as though he were running away from somebody, or something, which had scared him. His clothes were bespattered with mud. He had, in my opinion, a guilty look; and I am perhaps to blame for letting him pass by without a word. So I've come, sir, to ask your advice.'

The expression on Ludlaw's face suddenly changed.

'At what hour was this?'

'Between seven and eight.'

Ludlaw glanced at the clock on the mantelshelf. It was some minutes past ten.'

The situation disquieted Ludlaw. He had dined with Sir Michael Valroy at six o'clock. At seven the baronet had gone out. Had he again encountered Wildrake? Spicer's description of the man's appearance reminded him of Lady Valroy's words. She had heard of the unlucky meeting, and she had pleaded for permission to see her father, if only to appease his anger against the baronet. She had expressed a fear that his life was threatened. Ludlaw began to share her alarm.

'In which direction was Wildrake going?' he inquired.

'Towards London.'

'Could you point out the spot at which he passed you?'

'With the greatest ease.'

Ludlaw rose instantly from his armchair.

'Spicer,' said he, 'we will walk there together.'

'Then you think it serious, Mr. Ludlaw?'

'Very serious indeed.'

Hastily putting on his coat and hat, Ludlaw went into the night without another word, followed by Spicer. Along the avenue leading to the gates, quaint patches of moonlight, which had crept through the bare branches of the trees, lay in their path. The great solemn sphinxes, on each side of the gateway, had dark shadows on their stony faces.

But beyond, out on the common, the earth was as shadowless as though it were a moonlit sea. The two men issued forth out of the uncertain light and struck across the heath.

After walking nearly a mile, they came in sight of the clump of trees where Spicer had watched Wildrake unperceived.

'This,' said Spicer, when they reached the spot, 'is where I stood; and this,' he added, stepping out into the highway, 'is the direction Wildrake took. The road, as you see, runs east and west. He was going eastward, towards the City.'

'In that case,' said Ludlaw, 'let us go westward. But not so fast now. We must keep our eyes open and our ears too.'

Spicer glanced at the barrister keenly.

'Mr. Ludlaw,' said he, 'what do you suspect?'

'Foul play.'

'Murder?'

'That's the word.'

For some minutes they walked along in silence, keeping well in the centre of the road: there were no sounds except their footfalls—no shadow except their own which advanced before them, like phantom guides.

Presently Ludlaw looked at his watch. It wanted an hour of midnight. That Sir Michael was still abroad, the barrister had little doubt: for he had kept the pathways leading to the house well in sight, and not a single moving object had he yet seen. He listened unceasingly for the gate-bell, which, had it rung, would have reached his ear. His alarm increased at every step.

'Spicer,' he presently remarked, 'when I told you that I had grown suspicious about Wildrake, I referred to what I fear has now happened.'

'I understand, sir.'

'For many years,' Ludlaw pursued, 'Wildrake has had a real or imaginary grievance, I will not undertake to decide which, against Sir Michael Valroy. They lately met, as I have reason to know, on this very common: angry words have been exchanged between them, and even blows. It so chances that Sir Michael is out on the heath to-night: he has been out here since seven o'clock. Now it seems to me as a piece of very strong circumstantial evidence, judging from your description of Wildrake's appearance, that the two have met again. And Sir Michael,' added the lawyer, 'not having returned, leads me to fear that the issue has been disastrous.'

'That's what Mrs. Spicer thinks.'

'Wildrake,' said Ludlaw, 'is a dangerous character. His mind is disordered by drink. Having once got the notion into his head he would not hesitate to commit any crime—not even a murder.'

Spicer looked anxiously around.

'Should we not do well to give the alarm?'

'I have thought of that.'

'Have you a motive, Mr. Ludlaw, in taking this direction?'

'More motives than one.'

Coming to a broad path which curved to the left, out of the main road, Ludlaw arrested his steps and turned to Spicer.

'I have a fancy,' said he, 'to explore this corner.'

'I see your reason.'

'What is it?'

'On one side of that path,' said Spicer, 'there is a dark pool.'

'Well?'

'Wildrake's clothes were muddy: but the roads are dry.'

'Consequently . . .'

'That may be the spot.'

Ludlaw nodded and led the way. The path descended into a small valley, the sides of which were covered with thick bushes of brushwood and gorse. In the centre of this hollow lay a large pool, oblong in shape. The side of the pool which was bordered by the pathway was fenced off with white railings. The waste or overflow fell through an arched passage under the path into a rivulet not wider than a ditch. The sound of the water trickling into this rivulet reached them like a faint whisper. At the railings Ludlaw stopped and glanced about him. Then he looked down intently into the pool as though he would fathom its depth. But he only encountered a reflection of the crescent moon in an immeasurable profundity of bright sky.

'Is this pool deep?' he inquired of Spicer.

'Deep enough to drown a man.'

'Here? where we stand?'

'Anywhere, sir, within a foot or two of the bank. At this point, at the very edge, it's deep enough to drown a horse.'

They walked round the margin of the pool slowly, looking in every direction, and pausing at every step to listen or examine the ground. It was so swampy in many places that they sank up to their ankles in mud. But they both continued to advance, although they came upon no mark or evidence which could assist them in prosecuting their search. The reflection of the moon in the water followed their footsteps as they made the circuit of the pool; it seemed to regard them suspiciously, like a huge, half-closed eye.

They had once more reached the white railings, and were staring at each other with blank faces, when the noise of a horse's hoofs upon the road struck upon their ears.

'A swift animal,' Spicer remarked.

'Yes,' replied Ludlaw, 'and the very thing we need.'

He hastened up the path, by which they had come, leading to the highway. Spicer followed. In the distance they saw, on the moonlit road, a light dog-cart, in which were seated three men, coming towards them at a quick pace.

CHAPTER IX.

THE RECORD OF A CRIME.

CLOSING the journal, and locking the clasp, Paul Aldershaw replaced it in his drawer. For some minutes he sat quite motionless with a dark troubled look. He then touched his bell, and asked for Snowby.

The manager made his appearance.

'I should like,' said Paul Aldershaw, 'to have a few words with you, Snowby, when you have despatched the letters. It will not inconvenience you, I hope, to stop at the office half-an-hour or so later this evening?'

'Not in the least.'

'Very good. When you have dismissed the clerks, come to me.'

The merchant prince now began to busy himself with some papers on his desk before him. His face was thoughtful: he had suppressed the painful look. He was calm and statue-like.

'Are you at leisure now?' he demanded, looking up as Snowby stepped into the room.

'Perfectly, Mr. Aldershaw.'

'Be good enough, Snowby, to take a chair.'

The manager drew one forward, and, seating himself opposite to the merchant, waited for him to speak.

'I have serious thoughts,' began Paul Aldershaw, after a pause, ' of making some changes in the office. I find that my health will no longer support this constant wear and tear of City life; nor is it necessary, even supposing my nerves were stronger, that I should continue to give undivided attention to commerce. The affairs of the firm, as you have good reason to know, are in a very satisfactory condition; I have no desire to increase our connection at home or abroad. In fact, it would be advisable to consider whether, in the course of next year, we could not readjust affairs with foreign correspondents. But that is a matter of detail which we will reserve for discussion upon another occasion. I wish to consolidate the business, you will understand, rather than extend it.'

In this princely style he addressed his manager. A prime minister could scarcely have been more dignified, or formal, had he been making a statement to his secretary on affairs of state. Snowby listened attentively without offering to interrupt the merchant.

'First and foremost,' Paul Aldershaw continued, 'it must be distinctly understood that I have no intention of retiring. I shall ask you to take the helm, if I may so express myself, but I shall not leave the ship. In all probability I shall reside at Oaklands a great part of the year. That, however, is not a matter of certainty, nor is it of great importance, for wherever I am I shall have too much confidence in you to feel any anxiety. In fact, if I gave myself the slightest uneasiness I should be defeating my object. I am going to take things quietly,' added the merchant. 'I am in need of repose.'

He leaned back in his chair with his legs

crossed and his hands clasped together in his most statuesque attitude.

'Establish yourself,' he instructed his manager, 'in Mr. Grimwade's room. Get rid of the dust: re-arrange the document-boxes and old ledgers. That's the first thing to be done. I have no personal recollection of our late senior partner; but my father, I remember, always held him in high esteem as being very business-like and methodical; so it is high time we began to show some respect for his memory by putting his office in order. I am quite sure that you will do all in your power, Snowby, to prove yourself a worthy successor to Mr. Grimwade.'

'You may rely upon that, Mr. Aldershaw.'

'Well,' the merchant went on, taking a document from his desk, 'here, you see, is a rough draft of the deed which the lawyers have drawn up under my direction, with reference to this matter. You will have the right per procuration to sign for the firm. The concern will be carried on under your superintendence; a percentage of the profits, derived from the business, will be placed to your credit, and, independent of that, you will have the right to draw a specified sum per annum as manager. In fact, you will virtually occupy the position of junior partner in the house.'

'An enviable position indeed,' said Snowby.

'Possibly,' Paul Aldershaw acknowledged, with a look of pride; 'but not more than you merit. Your patience, tact, and intelligence could not be surpassed; your industry has been unflagging.

You have made yourself indispensable to me. That is the whole secret.'

The merchant smiled blandly, and handed the draft of the momentous document to Snowby.

'Examine this carefully,' said he, 'and then return it to me. If you have any amendments to suggest, I shall be ready and willing to consider them. That is all, I think, that I have to say on this subject to-night. Now, with regard to John Wildrake . . . What noise is that?'

'I heard nothing,' said Snowby, glancing about the room.

'You have dismissed the clerks?'

'Every one of them.'

'Very odd,' said the merchant. 'I am certainly under the impression that I heard some one in the office. My nerves must indeed be out of order. I must get away from town as soon as possible.'

'Shall I take a look round? Perhaps...'

'By no means,' Paul Aldershaw insisted, raising his hand. 'It is of no great moment whether there was a noise or not. What have you to report to me about Wildrake?'

'He is going from bad to worse.'

'You mean, he drinks more deeply?'

'No, Mr. Aldershaw,' said Snowby, with some hesitation.

'What then?'

'He has met the man,' said Snowby, 'against whom he has this supposed grievance.'

'Concerning his lost daughter?'

'Yes.'

That this daughter was an inmate of Snowby's house, and a different woman to what one imagined, was a secret which the manager could not disclose, even to the merchant, without committing a breach of confidence; and Paul Aldershaw, he was convinced, would have been the first to acknowledge this if placed in a similar position. This reflection relieved his conscience with regard to that portion of the affair which related to Madame Hélène.

But John Wildrake's attitude at the present moment was another matter: Snowby was accountable to the merchant, in a certain degree, for the old clerk's conduct. It was therefore his duty to repeat what he had recently heard from his vigilant friend Nedlicott about the man.

'Well?' said the merchant, with signs of anxiety.

'This meeting,' said Snowby, 'has distracted him. It has changed his character, his very mode of life. He has become a sober and uncommunicative person. He steals out after dark, no one knows where. He has not been seen at his favourite tavern for days. If he ever was bent on mischief, Mr. Aldershaw—if he ever was a danger to society, as you once yourself suggested, he is so now. For this man whom he has met, according to Wildrake's own account, struck him down without satisfying him about his daughter, and quitted him as he might have done a dog.'

The merchant looked up quickly, as though doubting if he had heard aright, and demanded:

'Did you say, "struck Wildrake down"?'

Before Snowby could reply, the door of

Mr. Grimwade's office, leading into Paul Aldershaw's room, slowly opened. The murky light from the crescent moon fell upon the threshold. John Wildrake appeared like an apparition. His face was ghastly, his eyes restless and unnaturally bright; he glared about him without seeming to fix his attention for an instant upon any object. His nervous fingers crept constantly over his features, or clutched at his torn and muddy clothes. His plight was pitiable and repulsive.

At sight of this weird figure, Paul Aldershaw sprang to his feet. The beating of his heart seemed arrested, and a chill crept through his veins; a dreadful thought had flashed upon him.

'Wildrake!' he exclaimed, in a broken voice, 'what does this mean?'

Wildrake stared at the merchant, and then bent his eyes to the ground, and passed his hand across his forehead. He offered no word of explanation; he looked as though his thoughts had been scattered by an overwhelming shock. The merchant again addressed him.

'Can I do anything for you?'

'Nothing.'

'Then why have you come here?' said Paul Aldershaw, 'and at this hour?'

Wildrake's eyes wandered, and he twitched more nervously still at the collar of his coat.

'That's the question,' said he, slowly, 'which I'm asking myself—why am I here to-night? Why, of all the wretched nights of my life, should I venture to come here on this one, the most wretched?'

He paused with an air of great trouble and perplexity.

'It's for the last time,' said he—'the last time. I'm going to take a journey. It's a long one—a very long journey, Mr. Aldershaw. I shall never come back.'

The merchant turned to his manager without hesitation.

'Snowby,' said he, 'provide John Wildrake with any money he may require . . .'

'No, no,' interrupted Wildrake, 'my journey is paid.'

Paul Aldershaw glanced keenly at Wildrake's face.

'Are you going to emigrate?'

'Yes, Mr. Aldershaw. You might call it emigration.'

'Why so?'

'Why? Because, sir, everything is found,' replied Wildrake, in a confused manner. 'Passage free.'

Again the merchant looked searchingly at his old clerk.

'When do you start, Wildrake, on this journey?'

'To-night. Can I have a word with you, sir, alone?'

The merchant made a sign to his manager to leave them.

The clerk's office had a dark and deserted appearance. Snowby returned to his desk and sat down. His mind was uneasy; he regretted being excluded from this interview. He had a presentiment of disaster. He could distinguish the voices of the merchant and his old clerk: broken words even reached him.

Wildrake's voice predominated. The tone was passionately excited. There were agonizing pauses; and when the merchant spoke it was only to utter a short and angry exclamation or remonstrance. Snowby's senses were therefore strung to a high nervous pitch.

Suddenly a shriek of horror came from Mr. Aldershaw's room.

Snowby leaped from his chair and ran in breathless.

The merchant was stretched upon the ground between his chair and the writing-table. He lay there a motionless heap with his hands tightly clenched above his head. Snowby threw a hasty glance around. There were no signs of any violence having been committed. The shaded lamp was burning steadily upon the table: not an article in the room was disarranged. Wildrake was standing with his hand on Mr. Grimwade's door. He cast a scared look at Snowby over his shoulder and disappeared. The look haunted the manager for days.

Lifting the merchant from the floor Snowby discovered that he was rigid and black in the face. He hastened to loosen his collar, and used every means in his power to revive him. Struggling for some moments as though with death, Paul Aldershaw began at last to show signs of consciousness. The colour returned to his cheeks and he opened his eyes.

'Where,' said he, grasping Snowby's arm, 'where is Wildrake?'

'Gone.'

'You have let him escape?'

Snowby explained to the merchant the situation in which he had found him. To have busied himself at such a moment with attempting to detain Wildrake, he averred, might have resulted in his (Mr. Aldershaw's) death.

'True,' he owned. 'How could you know?'

His voice was strangely agitated, and his hands trembled like a palsied old man's.

'Assist me to my carriage,' said he, rising in a feeble manner. 'I am rather shaken. I've received some startling news.'

Snowby gave the merchant his arm. They went down the staircase slowly. The moon was still visible, above the tall houses in the old square, and touched that side of the quadrangle upon which they came out. The other side lay in deep shadows. Paul Aldershaw shuddered as they issued forth into the gloomy night.

'The air is keen,' said he, peering nervously about. 'Is my carriage there?'

It was waiting outside the dark archway beyond the square. As soon as the merchant had taken his seat, he whispered hurriedly to Snowby, who stood at the carriage window:

'Take a cab. Drive post-haste to Scotland Yard. Bring a detective with you to my house. It is of vital importance that not a moment should be lost.'

'I understand.'

'It is a matter of life and death,' added Paul Aldershaw.

On descending from his carriage and stepping into the hall of his great Tyburnian mansion, the merchant observed Marion on the staircase. She looked at him wistfully, and then something in his face impelled her to hasten to his side. They went into Mr. Aldershaw's room together.

As soon as the door was closed he sank into his chair, near the fire, pale and shivering. Marion regarded him with alarm.

'Father,' said the girl, 'how ill you look!'

She took his hand: it was deadly cold and still trembling.

'Has anything happened?'

'Yes, Marion, something,' said he, deeply agitated,—'something which I would have given a fortune to prevent.'

And a look of agony crossed his face.

'I am expecting a visitor,' he presently added, rousing himself. 'I must brace my nerves for the interview. He may arrive at any moment.'

Marion proved herself devoted. Swiftly, but without a sound, she went in search of wine. She forbade a servant to enter the library. She brought her father his dressing-gown and slippers for the first time with her own hands, and tended him without an unnecessary word or movement. He rapidly recovered his usual composure: and it was only in his restless eyes that the active working of his brain now found expression.

There was a knock at the library door.

'At last,' said the merchant. 'Leave me, Marion.'

As Marion hastened from the room, Snowby stepped in, followed by a powerful-looking man with piercing black eyes and a black tuft of whisker under each ear—a typical detective.

The merchant motioned to his visitors to be seated.

'This evening,' said Paul Aldershaw, glancing at the detective, 'in fact, scarcely an hour ago, I received an extraordinary communication. Briefly, it is this.'

The detective took from a side pocket an oblong note-book. Detaching a pencil, he prepared, while making a table of his knee, to write his memoranda.

'Detained later than usual, at the office, with Mr. Snowby,' the merchant explained, with a wave of the hand towards his manager, 'I was interrupted in the midst of some business by a man, who, without any ceremony, walked into my room and asked leave to have a few words with me in private.'

The detective looked up from his notebook.

'Anyone, sir, of whom you had previous knowledge?'

'Yes: an old clerk.'

'What name?'

'John Wildrake.'

'Address?'

'Gable Court, Thames Street.'

The detective nodded.

'Well-known, sir,' said he, 'to the Force.'

'His appearance,' continued the merchant, 'roused my suspicions. His clothes were in rags and covered with mud. I agreed to hear, in private, what he had to say. At first I thought he must be out of his mind: his words were so like the ravings of a madman. But I soon had reason—being acquainted with John Wildrake's character—to change my opinion. His story was long and disconnected. To repeat it in detail now would be wasting precious moments. I will rapidly relate the mere substance of his disclosure without unnecessary detail or comment. You must accept it for what it is worth.'

The detective expressed his approval.

'This evening, about seven o'clock,' the merchant began, 'John Wildrake walks out, as he says, to Batswing Heath. There he descries Sir Michael Valroy—a man for whom he entertains a most deadly hatred. He has gone there in search of his enemy, and with the direct object of doing him bodily harm. He steps up behind him without a word or warning. Wildrake carries a heavy stick in his hand. At the very moment when Sir Michael Valroy turns and faces him he delivers his blow. He fells his victim like an ox, before he can grapple with his assailant, or before he can even stand on guard. In a word, Sir Michael Valroy is stretched upon the road on Batswing Common, in clear moonlight, dead at Wildrake's feet.'

The intensely earnest tone in which the merchant spoke, his contracted eyebrows, and his keen look fixed as though upon a dreadful vision of the scene which he was recounting, had a deep effect upon Snowby. He could scarcely have turned paler had he been witnessing the deed. The detective, perfectly unmoved, did not even raise his eyes from his note-book. His pencil even, although it became stationary, pointed towards the page upon which he had been writing, in readiness when Mr. Aldershaw should think fit to resume. The merchant hardly paused a moment.

'What happens then?' he resumed. 'John Wildrake, aghast at the situation, looks about him for a likely place in which to conceal this terrible evidence of his crime. He is at his wits' end. The large pool on the common, within view from where he stands, catches his eye. No doubt—as you will find if you go there—it conceals a secret in this still moonlit night. It is the sort of place which might be chosen for hiding some hideous handiwork. Wildrake quickly makes his choice. In a deep spot in this pool he sinks out of sight all traces of his deed.

The tragedy is played out. He then takes to flight. He reaches the City. Passing by the old square, in which he has spent his best days, he stops and enters. In a bewildered, half crazy state of mind he finds himself in my office. Seeing me there, his former friend, he makes this awful confession.'

The detective closed his note-book, dropped it into his side pocket, and rising quickly, said,

'You have nothing, sir, to add?'

'Nothing,' said the merchant, 'except to warn you that Wildrake is still at large.'

'Good-night, sir,' said the detective, stepping towards the door.

'One moment. You are going to make a search?'

'Yes.'

The merchant turned to Snowby.

'I would ask you, as a favour, to be one of the party. Can this be managed?' he added, addressing the detective.

'Certainly.'

The two men took their leave.

A light dog-cart awaited them at the corner of the square. Snowby mounted into a seat behind, and the detective placed himself beside the driver.

They went swiftly along in the direction which led towards the Thames. One of the bridges was soon crossed; and presently passing through a large suburb, south-west of London, they came out upon Batswing Heath.

Not a word was spoken during the drive. But Snowby, looking over his shoulder as they sped across the common, uttered an exclamation of surprise at seeing two men step into the middle of the moonlit road directly in their path.

These men as it will be surmised, were Ludlaw and the landlord of 'The Hunted Stag.'

CHAPTER X.

DRIFTED.

TED NEDLICOTT on his way home from the 'Frivolity' was arrested by the sound of voices at the gate-way of Gable Court. The voices were not loud—no more than excited whispers issuing from the open door of the old mansion. As Nedlicott hurried into the yard, with a sense of serious misgiving, Mr. Isaacs came out to meet him. The Jew had a scared look on his face.

'What is it now?' the secretary demanded.

'The worst,' said the Jew, wringing his hands, 'the worst that could possibly happen. He is accused of murder.'

'Wildrake?' exclaimed Nedlicott.

'Yes.'

'Where is he?'

'Upstairs. Hush!' said the Jew, lowering his voice. 'He has planned his escape. If he is guilty . . .'

The old man stopped.

'Well?'

'He will cheat justice.'

'How?'

The Jew put his face close to Nedlicott's, and uttered a few words in his ear.

Nedlicott started back and looked anxiously at Mr. Isaacs.

'So soon?'

'Yes. This time there is no hope.'

The two men stood upon the steps, outside the door, under the lamp, staring awestricken into each other's faces. Midnight struck, awakening low echoes in the court-yard. With the last stroke of the deep bell of St. Paul's, the City fell once more, as it seemed, into a dead repose; only on the river-side, among the barges, could be heard the muttering of the current in its rapid course. That tide was ebbing fast!

The house door being open, Nedlicott observed dark figures moving about in the hall and up and down the sombre staircase. A man in a thick top-coat, with piercing black eyes and a tuft of black whisker under each ear, came out and looked at him keenly and then went in again.

As this man disappeared, the Jew glanced at Nedlicott significantly. Nedlicott nodded and asked:

'Is Mr. Snowby here?'

'No.'

'I'll go for him,' said the secretary, 'at once.'

'That's right,' said Mr. Isaacs, approvingly. 'He will certainly be wanted.'

Nedlicott hastened out into Thames Street, and turned his steps towards Blackfriars. Engaging the first cab he met, he drove to Brixton in search of Mr. Aldershaw's manager.

On more than one occasion Nedlicott had remarked, when conversing with Snowby about Wildrake, that some important incidents connected with the old clerk's life were known to him—incidents about which he was evidently forced to guard silence. Snowby, he remembered, had only gone so far as to hint at the existence of some person or persons interested in Wildrake who would one day express their gratitude to him for having befriended a stranger by the wayside. Nedlicott was the last man to seek any such acknowledgment; but the fact that Mr. Aldershaw's manager was better acquainted with Wildrake's story—at least in earlier days—made it imperative that he (Nedlicott) should acquaint Snowby with everything which came under his notice regarding this unfortunate man. Would the news, thought Nedlicott, which he was conveying to-night be the last? It was greatly to be feared; and he dreaded to think what might be the issue of his visit on so tragic an errand as the one upon which he was now bent.

The little villa at Brixton, at this midnight hour, contained two watching, anxious women; for Snowby had not yet returned home. They were in Helen Valroy's room, where they had passed so many evenings together. Both were strangely silent and self-absorbed. Helen, full of inquietude, rose frequently and went to the window to look out into the leafless boulevard upon the cold moonlit night. Since the painful meeting with her husband in Ludlaw's chambers on the previous day, she had known no rest.

'Katie,' said she, 'that hideous presentiment about which I spoke to you this morning clings to me and grows stronger every moment. I cannot shake it off. I must go and see him, even to-night.'

Kate Snowby, seated at the table with

her face between her hands, turned her dreamy eyes towards her friend.

'At this late hour, Helen?'

'Yes; something urges me.'

'Wait. Father will return soon.'

'I cannot!' said Helen, rising hurriedly from her chair.

'Would you go alone?'

'I would do anything,' was the answer, 'to end this suspense.'

She passed into an adjoining room, and came quickly back with a hooded cloak thrown around her. Katie started up and placed a hand upon her arm.

'Helen! are you mad?'

'I shall be,' she replied, moving towards the door, 'if I stay here inactive any longer.'

Katie appealed to her in an earnest, supplicating tone.

'I implore—wait until father comes home. He may be there now; he may bring you news of him which will ease your mind. You have been so patient for weeks, dear Helen; be patient one hour more . . .'

'Another hour? It is an age. No; do not try to change my purpose. I have been weak and purposeless too long! I must not lose a moment now. What years I have wasted! and he has been listening and waiting for me all this while. You would not wish me, Katie, to reach his wretched garret when it is too late? That is what I most dread: it is the presentiment which has troubled me all day. Too late? It would be terrible.'

Deeply agitated, she once more laid her hand upon the door.

'Listen!' said Katie, springing towards

the window. 'Is not that the sound of wheels?'

'Yes!'

They stood side by side, holding each other in expressive silence. A vehicle driving rapidly up to the house: Katie lifted the curtain and looked down into the road. Some one stepped out and came quickly through the little gateway. Katie's heart beat fast.

'It's Mr. Nedlicott,' she whispered, recognising him in the moonlight. 'It's my Ned!'

'Alone?' said Helen, with a look of alarm; 'what can it mean?'

There was a low knock at the hall door.

'You shall soon know.'

Saying which, Katie fled down-stairs.

Helen Valroy sank into a chair with her head resting upon her hands. In this attitude, bewildered by anxious surmisings, she waited. She was as pale and motionless as a statue, her cloak still around her in agitated folds. Her eyes, which were feverishly bright, were fixed and stricken with a look of painful expectation: her face was startling in its tragic beauty: every line was reposeful yet full of life.

A few minutes passed and Katie returned. She came quietly beside her friend and sat down.

'Helen,' said she, ' dear Helen.'

Helen Valroy did not change her attitude; but she half closed her eyes as though listening with strange attention to the tone of Katie's voice.

'Mr. Nedlicott comes from Gable Court. Will you go back with him?'

Helen lifted her head suddenly and

looked with consternation into Katie's face.

'You do not dissuade me now?'

'No, not now.'

'Why not? Because he is dead?'

No, Helen. It is because . . .'

'What, Katie?'

The girl bent closely over her friend and said, in a low voice,

'Because the end is near.'

Without a word Helen rose from her chair. A slight shudder passed over her as she drew her cloak about her shoulders; then, moving quickly across the room, she followed Katie down-stairs.

An hour later—when the tide was still ebbing on its dark way past Gable Court—Helen Valroy hurriedly ascended the steps of the old mansion. Nedlicott was at her side, and they at once gained admittance at the hands of the watchful Jew.

Entering the dimly-lighted hall, Nedlicott spoke a word in Mr. Isaacs' ear, and then led the way up the dark, oaken staircase towards John Wildrake's room. The voices had ceased: the shadowy forms which Nedlicott had seen—even the man with the piercing black eyes—had disappeared. The Jew remained at the foot of the stairs stroking his long white beard, and with the far-off look in his pensive gaze.

On reaching the third-floor landing, Helen Valroy observed, in an obscure corner near the door, an uncouth, crouching form. The head was bent forward, and the long, tangled hair fell over the knees, which were tightly embraced by the two bare, long arms. This strange creature was shaken by stifled sobs. Helen stopped, and touched Nedlicott's arm.

'Who is this?' she whispered, with a look of wonder in her face.

'A waif,' said Nedlicott. 'She is called Mimosa.'

'Why is she crying?'

Nedlicott answered, in a low voice:

'He was kind to her. It must be for him—for John Wildrake.'

'Did she tend him, sometimes, do you think?'

'Yes, like a faithful slave.'

Helen knelt down beside Mimosa. Taking the girl's small, thin hand in hers, she bent gently over it. A tear fell upon the hand as she touched it with her lips. Then rising, she turned quickly away, and followed Nedlicott into Wildrake's chamber. The guttering candle was burning on the chest of drawers, feebly lighting up the miserable garret. Helen glanced despairingly around her. On the squalid bed, in his old, grey dressing-gown, lay John Wildrake, her neglected father. His head was thrown back on his right arm: the collar, wide open, exposed the throat, but he was breathing heavily, and his eyes were half closed. He looked like one in a profound and troubled sleep.

After gazing in amazement for some moments at this wretched figure, as though it were difficult of identification, Helen turned an appealing look at Nedlicott. He comprehended her meaning at once, and, moving towards the door, he went out, closing it softly behind him.

No sooner alone than Helen stepped swiftly to the bed-side, and threw herself down with a low and agonizing cry. The cloak, disengaged from her shoulders, fell in a whirl of folds at her feet. Her long arms encircled the sleeping figure: her eyes were fixed intently on the worn and wrinkled face.

The change in her father, since she had left her home to become the wife of Sir Michael Valroy, surpassed all expectation, although more than fifteen years had gone by. It was pitiable. Had she met him without previous warning, recognition would have been difficult indeed.

Wildrake stirred: low muttering sounds escaped his lips, which gradually formed themselves into words.

'Listen! Don't you hear it now? One moment, Ned: only one moment. She's coming back. That's my daughter's footstep. Hark! I never heard it so distinctly—never so distinctly as to-night. She's coming back at last.'

The muttering grew inaudible and the painful breathing continued, the eyes being still partly closed. Helen's regard was fixed upon her father's face with an intense expression.

Had he heard her enter his room? or was this raving, Helen wondered, the reminiscence of the footsteps which had haunted him for so many years? His brain was consumed by fever: she watched with eagerness every shadow of a change which passed over him. Presently Wildrake resumed, with a slight start,

'No, Mr. Aldershaw. No, sir, not that! I've a scheme for teaching the rising generation how to speak . . . the rising generation. I've taken a third-floor front. My landlord . . . I owe him money.

What I mean is . . . money. Eh? Has he faith in elocution? Not he! He's an ignorant Jew. He has asked me to pay my rent. What? That's what. I told everyone . . . happily married! No, no. She is lost. Do I know him? Do I know the man who has robbed me of my daughter? . . . Yes, that's his name: Sir Michael Valroy!'

A few unintelligible and broken sentences followed; and then for awhile he remained silent: as though the imaginary interview with the merchant prince had come to an end. But another scene began to exert its influence over his feverish fancy—a scene of stirring and tragic intensity. An exclamation escaped his lips, and he struggled into a sitting posture, and with his eyes wide open and as watchful as a hawk's. He stared as though a vision were rising up, and passing before him in the dimly-lighted room.

'Now,' he whispered, gasping for breath, and ghastly pale, 'now! It's my turn at last. He struck me down. Did he think to do that with impunity? I asked him for my daughter, and he struck me down! . . . How swiftly he walks! Does he suspect that I am close behind? . . . No, no. He does not look back . . . he suspects nothing. He shall not escape me . . . I have sworn that. There is no power that can hold my hand . . . there is no power. Hush! Does he hear? No . . . That's well. Softly . . . softly . . . now!'

He raised his right arm and aimed so vicious a blow at the air that he fell over with a groan on his left side. His whole expression was full of vindictiveness and destruction. Helen Valroy recoiled with a look of horror.

The vision was still in his eyes, but now as though directly below his feet.

'How the moonlight clings to his face! ... He's sinking, sinking fast. What shadow is that? Is it the black cloud over the pool? Ha! he is rising—rising out of the pool. Why is he dressed in white? Keep him down—keep him down. The water is red with his blood!'

He shrieked plaintively: then, falling back with a gasp upon his pillow, he lay silent and motionless. The terrified look in his eyes subsided, and the heavy breathing ceased: for the sleep John Wildrake had fallen into now was one out of which he would never awake. He had drifted: drifted at last beyond the sound of his daughter's footsteps—the footsteps which had haunted him for so many years.

Pacing up and down this dismal chamber—as though with those luckless footsteps she were essaying to re-animate her dead father, and wring from him a contradiction of her dreadful thoughts—Helen Valroy's face underwent a startling change. The tenderness of her expression vanished, and her beautiful features became hard and haggard, like the features of an old woman. Her eyes, a moment before flooded with tears, now flashed with passionate resentment and reproach, and the lines which crossed her forehead were fierce and unforgiving. She shrank back, shuddering each time she passed his bed. Her brain was throbbing madly, for she could not cast aside a conviction which had thrust itself upon her: the dead man seemed uttering the words:

Her husband is murdered: her father has done the deed.

Throwing her cloak once more around her with trembling hands, Helen Valroy fled from the room with one swift glance behind. The shock of her discovery had stricken her with a bewilderment more serious than the deepest grief: a terror had seized upon her which threatened to unhinge her mind, and destroy all rational reflection at the moment when it was needed most. She descended the staircase, listening at every step, with a piteous look of mental aberration gathering in her eyes. She met no one; but as she passed along the hall a light, issuing through a half-open door, attracted her attention. She peered into the room. It was a large work-shop, filled with frames, tablets, and other church decorations in an unfinished state. In this room she perceived Nedlicott and the old Jew standing over a low fire, and speaking together in subdued voices.

'Who told you this?' Nedlicott questioned the old Jew.

'The detective.'

'As being Wildrake's story?'

'His confession,' the Jew affirmed. 'The bad one openly avowed his crime to Paul Aldershaw.'

'There is no doubt . . .'

'None. The details have proved correct.'

'They have found Sir Michael Valroy?'

'Dead.'

'In the pool?'

'Yes; on Batswing Heath,' replied the

Jew. 'You remember the heavy stick which Wildrake carried about with him at night?'

'I remember.'

'That was his weapon. He killed Sir Michael Valroy with that.'

Helen waited to hear no more. She glided noiselessly along the hall. The front door was standing ajar, and she passed into Gable Court, her arms outstretched, as though she had been suddenly struck with blindness. Crossing the old yard with staggering footsteps, she stopped and leaned half swooning against the wall of a great warehouse at the riverside, among the shadows.

The sound of the ebbing tide, whispering around the dark barges, presently fell upon her ear. She uttered a low cry, and, turning with a sudden impulse, she approached the water's edge. She could see nothing below her feet: but from the lapping noise of the current against the bank, at the spot where she stood, Helen Valroy knew that with one step she could end all the misery and shame which had fallen upon her.

She had reached the brink, and was about to spring forward, when she felt two arms clasped round her figure like a vice. She was held forcibly back.

'Who's this?' she cried, struggling to free herself. 'I implore you, let me go.'

'Not me.'

'What is your name?'

'Mimosa. Do you know me now?'

'Yes.'

'Then listen! Let me die with you.'

'Why?' Helen demanded, in a tone of surprise.

'Because I liked him. I don't want to live.'

'Have you no friends?'

'Not now he's gone.'

'No home?'

'There's a cupboard on the staircase. It belonged to him: it's where he kept his lumber. That was my home. I've no home now.'

'Poor child!'

Helen Valroy stooped and placed her arms protectingly round the girl.

Mimosa knelt down at her feet and burst into tears.

'Don't cry, Mimosa. You shall have another home.'

'Near you?'

'Yes, near me: miles and miles away.'

'You do not wish to die?'

'No, no, please God, not now!'

She shuddered, and hastened from the river's edge, and out of the shadows.

Mimosa followed.

The tide had turned, and Helen Valroy was saved.

CHAPTER XI.

THE LAST ACT.

Years have gone by—three long years.

The great house of Aldershaw, Grimwade and Company still prospers. Paul Aldershaw, carrying out his project of dusting the late Mr. Grimwade's office, has instated Mr. Snowby there as junior partner: this plan enables the merchant prince to pass some months of the year at Oaklands, his country seat in Yorkshire.

Marion, more devoted than ever to her

father, cannot be induced to leave him, although she has had many brilliant offers of marriage.

There is no reserve between Marion and her father now—except on one subject: Roy Valroy.

Paul Aldershaw's character is altered. He is no longer the haughty, statuesque personage of former days. He has become natural: his manner is genial towards everyone. Even his interest in art has revived.

Snowby, who takes much credit to himself concerning this change, is deeply gratified; for he has, he believes, since his promotion, lifted a load off Mr. Aldershaw's shoulders. And whether Snowby's theory be true or false, as to his share in bringing about the merchant's rejuvenescence, no one denies, who knows anything about the great house, that the junior partner is the right man in the right place.

Snowby's dream of a mansion in Park Lane and a carriage and pair has dissolved. He begins to acknowledge (to himself) that Katie was right; the 'little place at Brixton' is good enough for him. He lives there all alone; for Katie and Nedlicott are married: but they rent a villa on the opposite side of the 'boulevard,' and there is another Katie there now who is often taken over, and sits on Snowby's knee, and puts her arms around his neck, just as Katie herself had done when she was a child.

Nedlicott, who has become part-proprietor of the 'Frivolity,' still superintends the production of Mr. Cheadle's comedies. Nor has Nedlicott's popularity at the

'Fresco' diminished. He sings his one great song there (for the members will not hear of any 'change of programme') every Saturday evening with rounds of applause. Snowby has been elected a member of the club: but that gentleman's dignified position, as partner in the house of Aldershaw, will no longer permit him to own that he has a voice. He has never been known to sing a song, even at home, since the deed of partnership has been signed.

Nedlicott's mother, who has not yet quite forgiven Katie for taking her son away from her, still looks out through the glass window of her snug parlour for the shadows of customers. And scarcely a day passes without the shadow of the old Jew darkening the threshold; for he looks in to have his snuff-box replenished, and to gossip with Mrs. Nedlicott about his lodgers: and sometimes, when shaking his head over some troublesome 'floor' in Gable Court, who happens to be in arrears with his rent, he is reminded of the 'bad one,' and his gaze becomes distant and melancholy. That eccentric lodger and all his tragic surroundings can never be forgotten.

Helen Valroy leads a restless life abroad. She corresponds with Katie; but her letters are seldom dated from the same town. She is sometimes in Italy, sometimes in Switzerland, sometimes in France. Mimosa travels with her. That late inhabitant of Gable Court, now that the black patches have been permanently removed from her face, exhibits signs of beauty; and, under Helen's careful supervision, she is developing some brain power which was not supposed to exist during the Gable Court period of her existence.

Another, though less frequent correspondent of Helen Valroy's is Ludlaw. In his matter-of-fact, business-like manner, he continues to show himself her friend. He has, in fact, the same kind of affection for old clients which he has for old deeds. Surrounded by these documents in Pump Court, he has only to glance around him to recal to mind the 'causes' in which he has pleaded eloquently any time these twenty years. That he has a fine, original intellect nobody ever doubts; but his 'system of order' is one which cannot be explained to any person's satisfaction except his own.

Ludlaw—as he sits one morning over

his breakfast and cigarette at his chambers in Pump Court—looks the same as he did three years ago. It is true that his hair is touched with grey, and that the crowsfeet at the corners of his eyes are becoming pronounced. But these 'shadings' give an expression of increased shrewdness to his face.

Presently a knock at the staircase door brings a flash of expectation to the lawyer's eyes. He rises hastily, and stands in a listening attitude.

There is a quick step in the passage, and the door opens, and a handsome fellow, with a sunburnt face, springs into the room.

'My learned friend!'

'Ludlaw! How are you?'

The two men shake hands very heartily,

and then look at each other with searching eyes.

'So,' declares Ludlaw, 'you have come back to England at last!'

'Yes; at last.'

'That's well,' asserts the lawyer. 'You have acted wisely. You will win her now.'

'Is it possible that Marion . . .'

'Quite possible. She's not married yet.'

Roy sinks into Ludlaw's chair. Since his parting with Marion at the Cheadles' house in Chelsea, three years ago, he has never once set foot in England. He has become a famous traveller; the most unfrequented regions of Asia, Africa, and America have been explored by him. He has escaped death a dozen times, and, of course, in a dozen different ways. Reckless in adventure, he has sought rather than avoided danger. Life without Marion was valueless to him.

At length news reached him—news that was many months old—relating how Viscount Dwyver, Lord Mounthaw's only son, was drowned. He had been caught in a storm off the Irish coast, while cruising with his yacht, and all hands on board had perished.

A year passed: and then came news of the death of the Earl of Mounthaw. He was reported never to have recovered from the shock which he had sustained on hearing of his son's loss. Lady Mounthaw survived her husband only a few months.

Roy Valroy, thus finding himself unexpectedly the owner of Mounthaw, resolved to return at once to England.

'I have travelled, Ludlaw, night and day from Marseilles. Did you get my telegram?'

'Yes. I expected you this morning.'

'Ah! Shall we start to-day for Mounthaw?'

'This afternoon,' Ludlaw replies. 'You must submit to an interview with the late earl's solicitors before you leave town. I have made an appointment for you at eleven o'clock in Lincoln's Inn.'

'Many thanks. Now give me something to eat and tell me all the news. How like old times! Do you remember our days here together when I was first called to the Bar? Ah, Ludlaw, what an age it seems: and yet I am still young!'

Next morning—a bright midsummer's morning in July—Roy Valroy is walking briskly across the fields from Mounthaw, and soon reaches the home park leading to Oaklands.

Paul Aldershaw's mansion comes in sight when Roy turns into the old avenue—an avenue of elm-trees nearly a mile in length.

His heart beats wildly at the thought of meeting Marion once more. Will she have forgotten? That is the one question which he repeats to himself a hundred times. Will she have forgotten?

As he approaches the house—a fine Elizabethan structure—a gentleman appears in sight and advances to meet him.

'My hero! why,' he exclaims, 'I do declare—from a dramatic point of view—this is the situation I am waiting for. You have saved the comedy!'

'Have I, Cheadle?'

'Have you? Why, I'll undertake as soon as you like to ring down the curtain! Act the fifth: scene—avenue: mansion in the background. Enter hero . . .'

'Now, Cheadle, be serious. How is . . .?'

'Marion? In perfect health, and more lovely than ever!'

'Does she know?'

'Of course! Why, every man, woman, and child, within ten miles of Oaklands knew of your arrival last night.'

'But, Cheadle . . .'

'Well?'

'Do you think that Mr. Aldershaw, as a neighbour, will receive me?'

'What a question! Now, how can I—from a dramatic point of view—give you an answer? It would spoil the play.'

Silence ensues. Roy walks beside the incorrigible dramatist towards the house. They cross the lawn, and a flower-garden, and enter a boudoir through open windows. There they discover Ada Cheadle, in an arm-chair, fast asleep. She has not changed.

'Ada, my dear,' says Mr. Cheadle, rousing his wife. 'Here's our old hero, Valroy!'

Ada shakes hands with Roy in a languid manner, and very much as she would have done had she met him only the day before.

'Will you tell Marion?' says Mr. Cheadle, as soon as a few words have been exchanged between Valroy and his wife. 'Will you tell Marion that Roy is here? We must not forget our heroine.'

Ada rises, and with a languid smile leaves the room; but she moves so slowly that Valroy is almost tempted to rush out before her and announce himself with a shout.

'And now,' Mr. Cheadle remarks, stepping towards the windows. 'I'll retire. It's more dramatic. What's the next scene? Meeting between hero and heroine after a lapse of three years! I shall be ready to ring down the curtain soon: you leave all that business to me.'

With these words Mr. Cheadle makes his exit, and Valroy finds himself alone.

It is an anxious moment. Roy Valroy's heart beats faster still. The minutes seem like hours. Will she never come?

The door opens at last, and Marion steps into the room. She holds out her hand hesitatingly as he advances towards her. The greeting is like that of friends —not of lovers—except that both are silent.

'You are at Mounthaw now.'

'Yes: at Mounthaw.'

'Have you been long in England?'

'Since yesterday.'

Roy Valroy, gaining courage, begins to study Marion's face. He sees a change which pains him. She is no less beautiful now than when they parted; but her face is thin and more pale; and there is in her eyes a look as though of weariness through watching too closely the flight of years.

Roy ventures to inquire, 'Is Mr. Aldershaw well?'

'Quite well,' Marion replies. 'He is away from home.'

'In London?'

'Yes; on City affairs,' says Marion. 'He does not return for some days.'

Not for some days! Roy Valroy can scarcely conceal his disappointment. The merchant prince's absence means delay. He had walked over from Mounthaw picturing to himself a satisfactory interview with Paul Aldershaw; and then a delightful scene with Marion—a scene of love such as he had known in the old days after their meeting by the sea. He had pictured her springing into his arms—or at least bursting into tears: he had forgotten that three years had passed since they parted. But her calmness and dignity teach him to realize the length of time to its utmost now.

Taking leave of Marion, after lingering for a while, he wanders back to Mounthaw over the fields, strangely depressed and wishing that he had remained abroad.

And yet he cannot find, in his heart, that Marion has been colder towards him than he has been towards her. She had not refused to see him; and could he expect a different reception after the lapse of years? They had been lovers once; but that was all ended long ago by mutual consent.

Roy waits, by Ludlaw's advice, until the merchant prince shall return to Oaklands.

Some days pass. Roy is growing impatient. But one morning, on returning home from a drive with Ludlaw across the park, he finds a note in Marion's handwriting. It is an invitation to dinner at Oaklands; Mr. Aldershaw has returned.

Valroy remains all that summer at Mounthaw; and scarcely a day passes without a visit to Oaklands. He and Marion become lovers once more; and after this second wooing—more passionate than the first—Marion is won.

In the following spring, Roy Valroy, Earl of Mounthaw, and Marion Aldershaw are married. All the tenants on the two estates are invited to the wedding.

Thus the ambitious projects which the merchant prince had once planned are at last fulfilled, not only to his heart's content, but to the content of all those who are loved by him at Mounthaw.

THE END.

www.ingramcontent.com/pod-product-compliance
Lightning Source LLC
Chambersburg PA
CBHW032104220426
43664CB00008B/1127